HAL LEONARD
GUITAR METHOD

Supplement to Any Guitar Method

FOLK GUITAR

BY FRED SOKOLOW

PLAYBACK+
Speed • Pitch • Balance • Loop

To access audio visit:
www.halleonard.com/mylibrary

Enter Code
4610-4831-0012-5631

with editorial assistance by Ronny Schiff

All instruments played by Fred Sokolow
Recorded at Sossity Sound by Michael Monagan

ISBN 978-1-4584-0241-7

7777 W. BLUEMOUND RD. P.O. BOX 13819 MILWAUKEE, WI 53213

Visit Hal Leonard Online at
www.halleonard.com

CONTENTS

INTRODUCTION

This book and accompanying audio will get you started playing folk music. You'll learn several backup techniques and soloing strategies, enabling you to play many different types of tunes with a variety of rhythmic grooves. Along the way, you'll learn a whole slew of songs made popular in the "folk era" of the late 1950s and mid 1960s—when folk music, for a brief time, merged with pop music.

Player's note: The accompanying audio contains play-along tracks and musical examples of the patterns and techniques that are presented in the book. All guitar parts are panned to the right side of the stereo mix so that you can isolate them for close study or pan them out for playing along with the band.

WHAT IS FOLK MUSIC?

What is "folk music"? To paraphrase Pete Seeger, they used to call it *folk* music if an old-timer, sitting on a porch somewhere in the hills, was singing a song that his grandparents taught him—a tune so old that nobody knew who wrote it—and strumming a banjo or some other stringed instrument. Nowadays it's folk music if a young girl is playing an acoustic guitar plugged into an amplifier on a stage in front of a paying audience, singing a song she wrote last week. The legendary trumpeter, Louis Armstrong, summed it up this way: "I never saw a horse that could sing, and I reckon all the songs sung by folks, instead of horses, are folk songs."

The truth is that the term "folk music" encompasses many things, including both "Americana" forms like bluegrass, old-time string-band music, country blues, or Cajun, as well as contemporary singer-songwriter music that is acoustic guitar-driven and makes some musical reference to Americana styles. That could mean rural folks like Elizabeth Cotten, Mississippi John Hurt, Woody Guthrie, or Doc Watson; it could also mean urban folkies like Pete Seeger and Joan Baez or singer-songwriters like Bob Dylan and Ben Harper. It could include Kurt Cobain performing a Leadbelly tune or Jack White singing and playing his version of a Son House blues.

If you like blues, bluegrass, old-time music, folk-pop, folk-rock, indie, or that all-inclusive term "Americana," you'll find a wealth of songs and guitar tips in the pages that follow. All of the tunes and exercises in the book are played on the accompanying audio to enhance your learning experience. A glance at the songs listed in the contents page will tell you all you need to know about the repertoire that's in store.

Good luck!

Fred Sokolow

Fred Sokolow

WHAT TYPE OF GUITAR TO USE

You can play any guitar you like and still be a folk musician. There are no rules, but there are conventions; acoustic guitars are more associated with the genre than electric guitars, though many people play acoustic/electric guitars (which are acoustic guitars with a built-in electric pickup). They can be plugged into an amplifier or sound system or played "unplugged."

Bluegrass and old-time (traditional) players, as well as blues players, prefer steel-string guitars rather than nylon-string guitars. (Many blues players prefer resonator guitars that have metal bodies, such as National guitars.) Many folks prefer the twelve-string guitar, which has six pairs (or *courses*) of strings. It's played just like a six-string, but it has a richer sound.

| Martin D-28 | Nylon-String Guitar | 12-String Guitar | All-Metal National |

FLATPICKS AND FINGERPICKS

You don't have to use picks at all, but they make your guitar tone louder and brighter, and if you play with other people (sans picks) for any length of time, you may have sore fingers!

Bluegrassers and other strummers usually use a flatpick, while fingerpickers (especially in the blues vein) often wear a thumb-pick (usually plastic) and one or two metal fingerpicks. A heavy flatpick that doesn't bend is preferred. Here are some of the more popular pick shapes and how they're held (or worn):

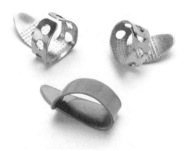 

Fingerpicks and Thumb-Pick

Various Flatpicks

Wearing Picks

Holding Pick

Thumb-picks come in different sizes, and metal fingerpicks can be bent to fit different size fingers.

ACCOMPANIMENT

Learning basic accompaniment is a good way to begin learning folk (or just about any style of music) even if your goal is to be a hot soloist. While learning backup, you'll acquire the chords, bass runs, rhythmic strums, and picking patterns needed to play solos and accompany vocals. Besides, unless you plan to play instrumentals exclusively, you'll probably spend more time playing backup than soloing.

STRUMMING

Strumming is brushing down on all or most of the strings of a stringed instrument with a pick or with your fingers and thumb. Guitarists often strum a repetitious one- or two-bar pattern to accompany their voice. Songs have different rhythmic feels, such as a shuffle beat, straight-eighth (rock) feel, waltz time, and so on. There's at least one strumming pattern for each of these feels.

Basic Strum

Here's a basic strum that suits many different types of tunes. The ⊓ represents downstrokes and the ∨ represents upstrokes. You can strum with a flatpick, fingernails, or your thumb for the downstrokes and your thumbnail for the upstrokes. However you decide to strum, there are four beats, and there's a pause after the first beat. Listen to the recorded track and you'll hear that the strum works for a song with a moderate or bright shuffle beat; it can also have a folk-rock (straight-eighth) feel.

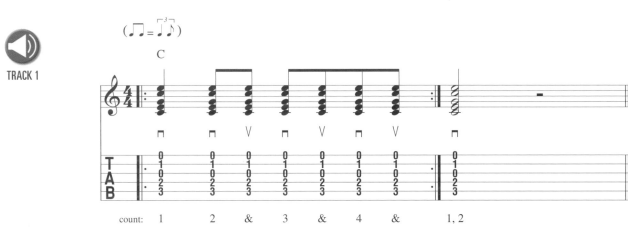

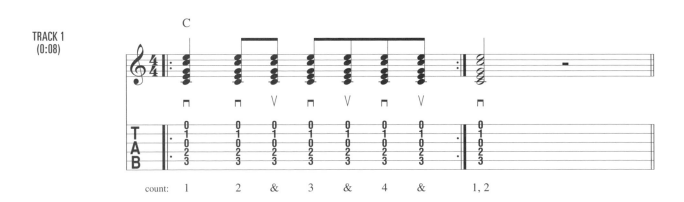

Here are two verses of "If I Had a Hammer," showing both types of rhythm. An anthem of the civil rights movement, the song was written by Pete Seeger and Lee Hays (of the Weavers) and first recorded in 1949. Peter Paul & Mary made it a pop hit in the 1960s, and Trini Lopez's rock version was also a million-seller a few years later. This arrangement is based on the Weaver's version.

IF I HAD A HAMMER (THE HAMMER SONG)

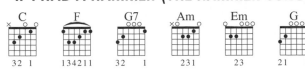

Shuffle feel

Verse

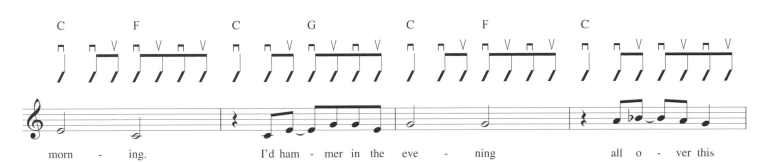

1. If I ___ had a ham - mer, ___ I'd ham - mer in the

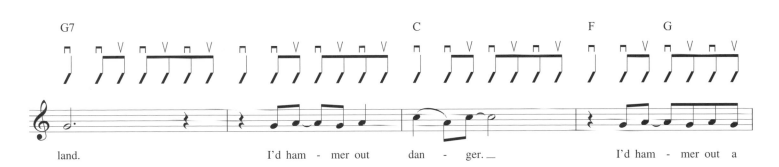

morn - ing. I'd ham - mer in the eve - ning all o - ver this

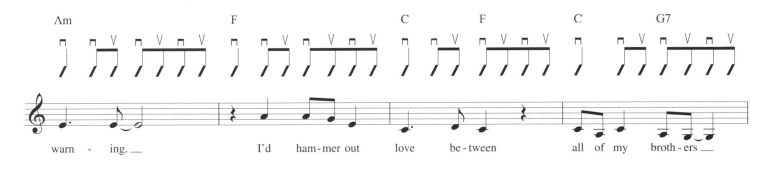

land. I'd ham - mer out dan - ger. ___ I'd ham - mer out a

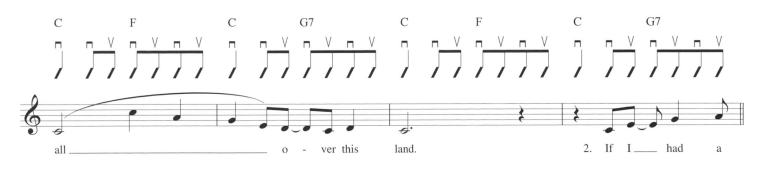

warn - ing. ___ I'd ham-mer out love be - tween all of my broth - ers ___

all _____ o - ver this land. 2. If I ___ had a

7

Verse
Straight-Eighth feel (♪♪ = ♪♪)

Additional Lyrics

3. If I had a song, I'd sing it in the morning. I'd sing it in the evening, all over this land.
   I'd sing out danger. I'd sing out a warning.
   I'd sing out love between my brothers and my sisters all over this land.

4. Well, I've got a hammer, and I've got a bell, and I've got a song to sing all over this land.
   It's the hammer of justice; it's the bell of freedom.
   It's a song about love between my brothers and my sisters all over this land.

In "Michael Row the Boat Ashore," the same strum has a lazy, almost ballad-like feel. This song was sung by freed slaves on the sea islands of South Carolina during the Civil War and was brought into the folk repertoire in the 1950s. Folksinger Bob Gibson performed it on a *Live at Carnegie Hall* album, and in 1961, the folk group the Highwaymen sang it all the way to #1 on the pop charts.

TRACK 2

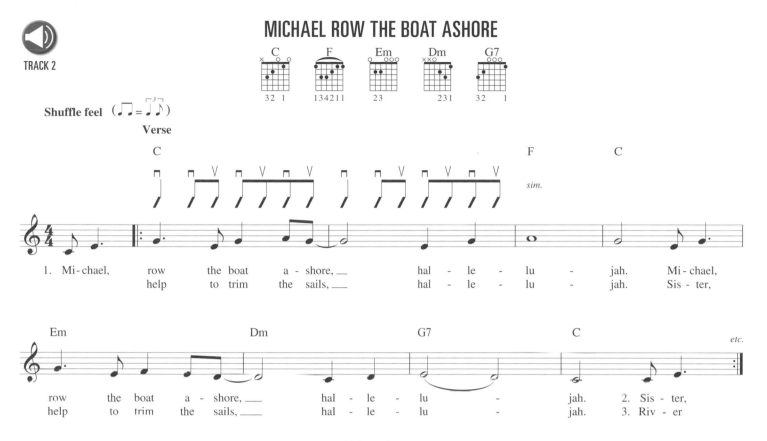

Additional Lyrics

3. River Jordan is chilly and cold, hallelujah.
   Chills the body but not the soul, hallelujah.
4. Jordan river is deep and is wide, hallelujah.
   I've got a home on the other side, hallelujah.
5. Michael's boat is a music boat, hallelujah.
   Michael's boat is a music boat, hallelujah.

Calypso Strum

By altering the basic strum just slightly, it takes on a *calypso feel. In the strumming pattern below, there are two pauses instead of one. To get the right rhythmic feel, strum up and down four times in each measure (which totals eight strums over four beats) but deliberately miss the strings on the second and fifth strums (the first upstroke and the third downstroke).

TRACK 3

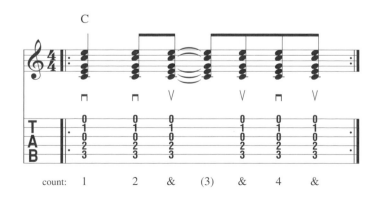

* The rhythmic music from Trinidad called "calypso" entered the U.S. pop charts in the 1950s. In 1956, Harry Belafonte's "Banana Boat Song" sparked a calypso craze that spawned many hit songs and movies.

Try the calypso strum on "Sloop John B.," a West Indies folk song that poet/folk song collector Carl Sandburg discovered in 1927. Most people know the song from the 1966 Beach Boys' hit. Their version was based on the 1958 recording by the Kingston Trio—one of the main folk groups that sparked the folk craze of the late 1950s and early 1960s.

TRACK 3
(0:10)

SLOOP JOHN B.

Verse

1. We come on the Sloop John B., my grand - fath - er and me. A-
   hoist up the John B.'s sail. See how the main sail sets.

round Nas - sau town ___ we ___ did roam. Drink - ing all
Call for the cap - tain a - shore, let ___ me go home. Let ___ me go

night, got in - to a fight. I
home, I wan - na go home. I

feel so break ___ up, I wan - na go home. 2. So,
feel so break ___ up, I wan - na go home. 3. The

Additional Lyrics

3. The first mate he got drunk and broke in the captain's trunk.
   The constable had to come and take him away.
   Sheriff John Stone, why don't you leave me alone?
   This is the worst trip I've ever been on.

Waltz Strum (3/4 Time)

Here's a strum pattern for waltz tunes, or songs in 3/4 time. It includes a pause after the first downstroke:

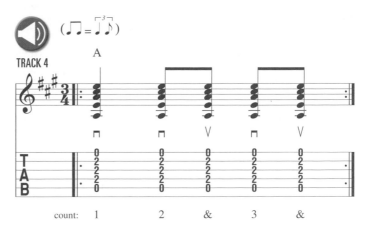

Try the waltz strum on "Little Boxes," a song about urban sprawl made famous by Pete Seeger in 1963, but written by folk-singer/songwriter Malvina Reynolds—she also wrote "What Have They Done to the Rain?" (about nuclear fallout) and the children's songs "Magic Penny" and "Morningtown Ride." Reynolds wrote one song every day! "Little Boxes" found a new audience in the mid 2000s when it was used as the opening song for the TV series, "Weeds."

TRACK 4
(0:06)

LITTLE BOXES

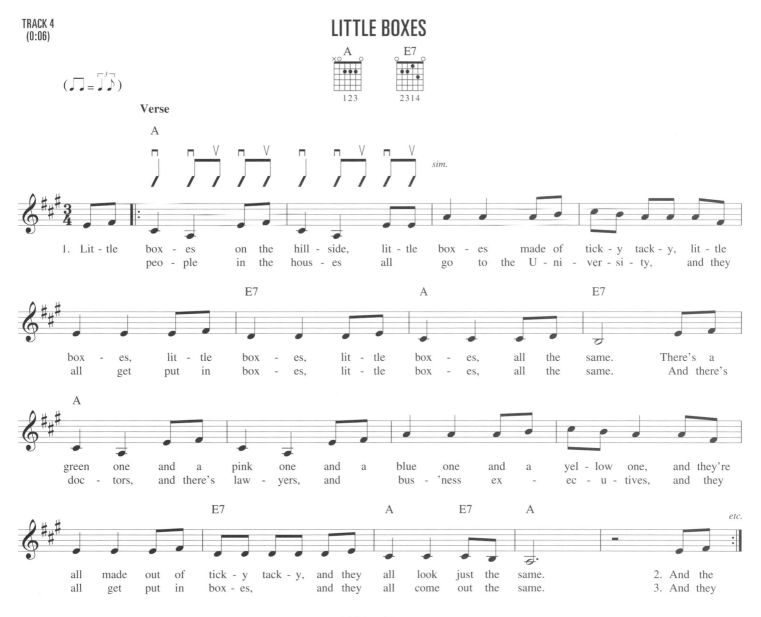

Verse

1. Lit-tle box-es on the hill-side, lit-tle box-es made of tick-y tack-y, lit-tle
   peo-ple in the hous-es all go to the U-ni-ver-si-ty, and they

box-es, lit-tle box-es, lit-tle box-es, all the same. There's a
all get put in box-es, lit-tle box-es, all the same. And there's

green one and a pink one and a blue one and a yel-low one, and they're
doc-tors, and there's law-yers, and bus-'ness ex-ec-u-tives, and they

all made out of tick-y tack-y, and they all look just the same. 2. And the
all get put in box-es, and they all come out the same. 3. And they

Additional Lyrics

3. And they all play on the golf course and drink their martinis dry,
   And they all have pretty children and the children go to school.
   And the children go to summer camp and then to the university,
   Where they're put in boxes and they come out all the same.

4. And the boys go into business and marry and raise a family
   In boxes made of ticky tacky and they all look just the same.
   There's a pink one and a green one and a blue one and a yellow one,
   And they're all made out of ticky tacky and they all look just the same.

6/8 Time Strum

Many popular songs have a 6/8 time signature, which means that there are six beats per measure. Here are two nearly identical 6/8 strums. One consists of six downstrokes, and the other has a single upstroke to give it some syncopation.

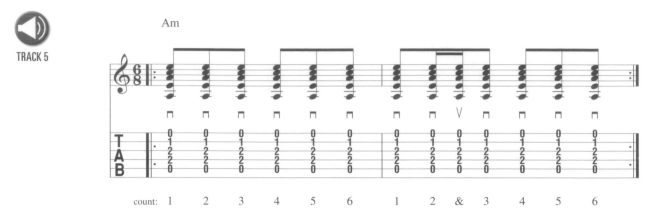

TRACK 5

"The House of the Rising Sun" is a well-known 6/8 time folk song. Another is "Greenfields," a #2 hit on the 1962 pop charts for the folk group the Brothers Four. The melancholy tune was penned by Frank Miller—a member of a popular 1950s folk group called the Easy Riders. Here is an excerpt starting at the bridge before the third verse.

TRACK 5
(0:09)

GREENFIELDS

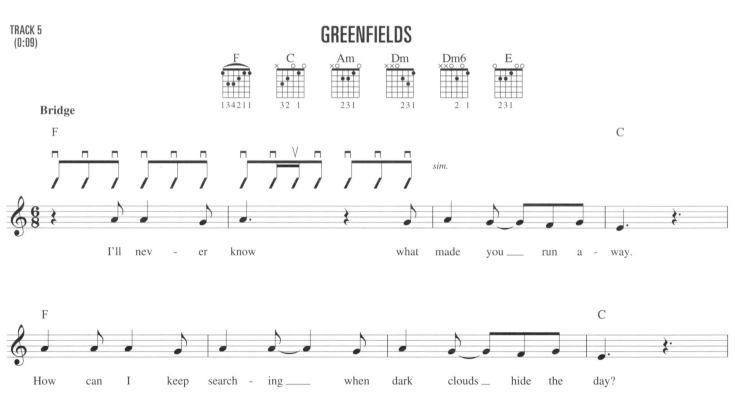

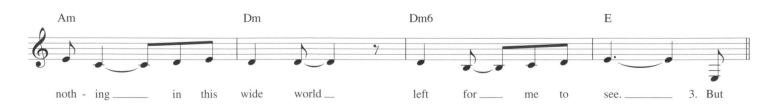

Verse

I'll _____ keep on wait - ing _____ 'til you re - turn.

I'll _____ keep on wait - ing _____ un - til the _____ day you learn

you _____ can't be hap - py _____ while your heart's _ on the roam.

You _____ can't be hap - py _____ un - til you _____ bring it home,

home to the green fields _____ and me _____ once a -

gain. _____

Additional Lyrics

1. Once there were green fields kissed by the sun.
   Once there were valleys where rivers used to run.
   Once there were blue skies with white clouds high above.
   Once they were part of an everlasting love.
   We were the lovers who strolled through green fields.

2. Green fields are gone now, parched by the sun.
   Gone from the valleys where rivers used to run.
   Gone with the cold wind that swept into my heart.
   Gone with the lovers who let their dreams depart.
   Where are the green fields that we used to roam?

FLATPICKING — CARTER STYLE

Flatpicking means strumming or picking individual strings of a stringed instrument with a pick. Many guitarists employ a flatpicked accompaniment style made famous by Maybelle Carter of the legendary folk group the Carter Family. Her soloing and accompanying styles have been widely imitated since she and the Carter Family rose to fame in the early 1930s.

The Basic Carter Lick

1. Pick the root bass note (for example, the sixth string/third fret in a G chord).

2. Brush down on the top three or four strings.

3. Brush up on the top three or four strings.

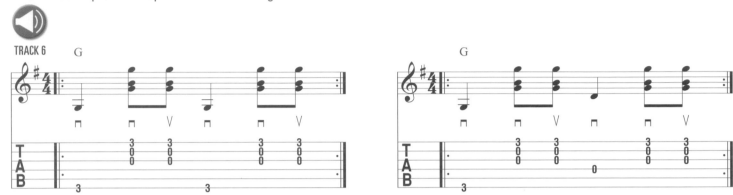

Notice that the second musical sample has an *alternating bass*. The single bass note alternates between the *root* and *5th*. The *root* is the note that gives the chord its name (such as G in a G chord); the *5th* is the fifth note of the major scale (such as D—the fifth note in the G major scale). The alternating bass is the standard Carter-style accompaniment.

"I Am a Man of Constant Sorrow" (below) affords a perfect example of Carter-style accompaniment; the basic Carter lick is used throughout. The song was first written down in 1913, but it was probably composed before then. The Stanley Brothers recorded it in 1951, and Bob Dylan recorded it on his first album in 1962.

I AM A MAN OF CONSTANT SORROW

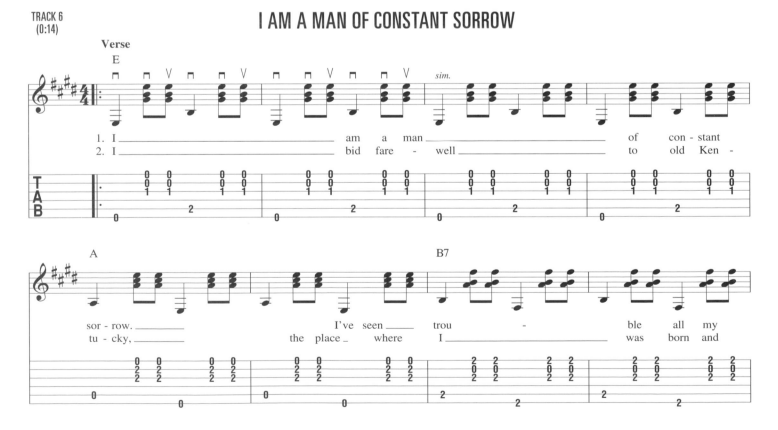

days.
raised.

The place where

he _____ was born and raised.

Additional Lyrics

3. For six long years I've been in trouble. No pleasure here on Earth I find.
   For in this world I'm bound to ramble. I have no friends to help me now.
   He has no friends to help him now.

4. It's fare you well my own true lover. I never expect to see you again.
   For I'm bound to ride that northern railroad. Perhaps I'll die upon this train.
   Perhaps he'll die upon this train.

5. You may bury me in some deep valley, for many years where I may lay.
   Then you may learn to love another while I am sleeping in my grave.
   While he is sleeping in his grave.

6. Maybe your friends think I'm just a stranger. My face you never will see
   But there is one promise that is given: I'll meet you on God's golden sho
   He'll meet you on God's golden shore.

Bass Runs

Guitarists playing Carter-style backup often use bass runs to connect one chord to another. These short phrases are usually based on the major scale from the song's key. Here are some typical bass runs:

TRACK 7

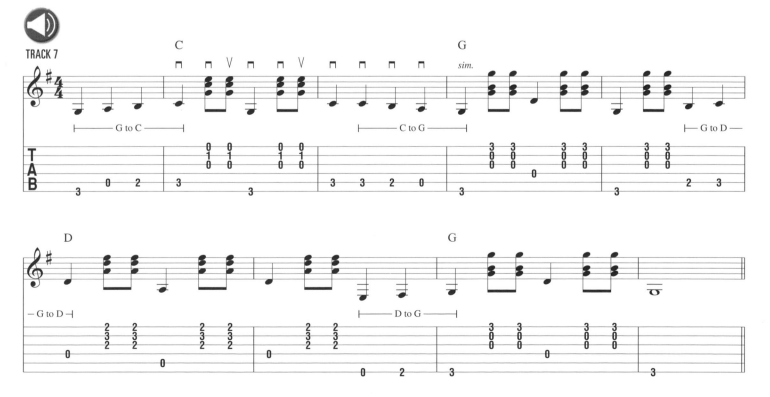

"Tom Dooley" is a study in bass runs. It also affords a good example of how urban folkies typically altered an old Appalachian folk song. Tom Dula, a North Carolina Civil War veteran, was hanged in 1868 for murdering a woman with whom he was involved (in a love triangle). The "other woman" was probably the real murderer, but the resulting song made Dula a legend. Rural Appalachian players played the tune with a Carter-style approach. In 1958, the Kingston Trio's urbanization of the tune was a huge pop hit. They simplified the melody and gave the song a neo-calypso swing. They also added a catchy syncopation with a pause just before "Dooley" in the vocal line.

In the version below, the chorus resembles the Kingston Trio's arrangement, and the next verse is in the Carter style with several bass runs. The next two verses are in different keys—in order to demonstrate additional bass runs. Here's the strum used in the Trio's version.

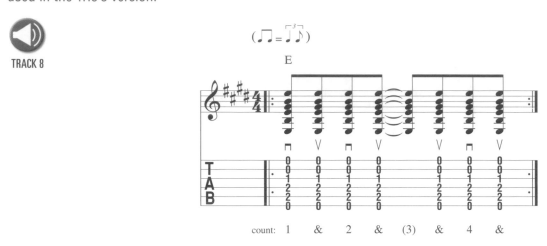

TOM DOOLEY

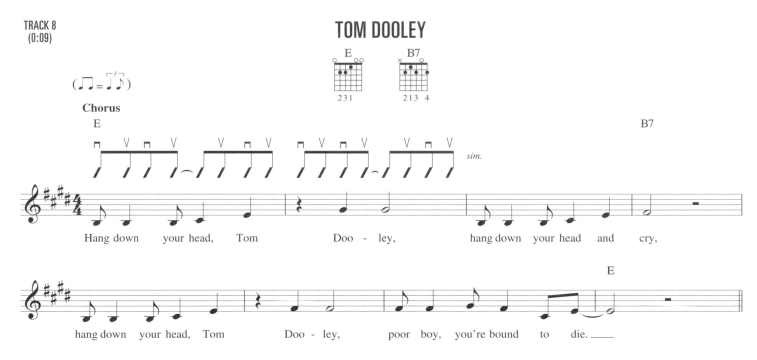

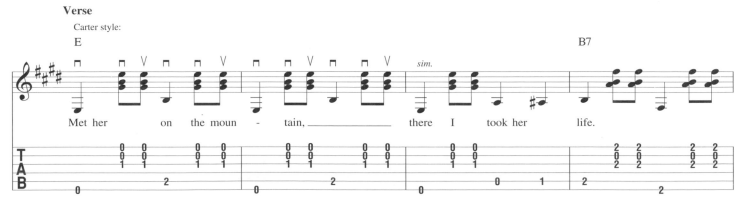

Words and Music Collected, Adapted and Arranged by Frank Warner, John A. Lomax and Alan Lomax
From the singing of Frank Proffitt

Met her on the moun - tain, stabbed her with my knife.

Verse

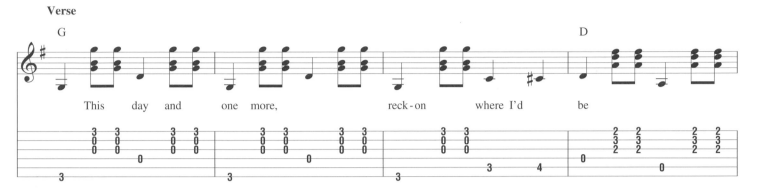

This day and one more, reck-on where I'd be

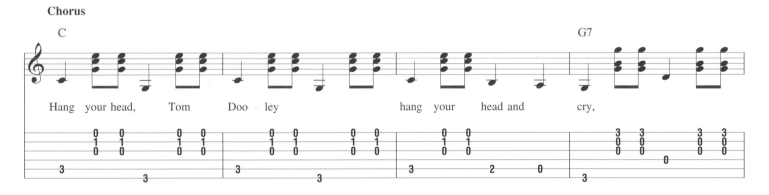

had-n't been for Gray - son, I'd been in Ten-nes - see.

Chorus

Hang your head, Tom Doo - ley hang your head and cry,

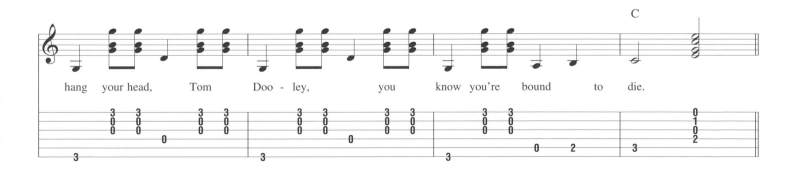

hang your head, Tom Doo - ley, you know you're bound to die.

The Carter-Style Waltz

If you change the first stroke of the waltz strum (Track 4) to a single bass note, you have a Carter-style waltz strum. To do this:

1. Pick a bass note.

2. Strum down on the treble strings (first, second, and third strings).

3. Strum up on the treble strings.

4. Repeat steps 2 and 3.

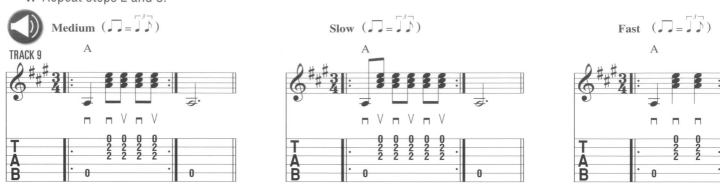

The faster strum is simplified by eliminating the upstrokes. Here's a verse of "Little Boxes" that makes use of the Carter-style waltz strum.

TRACK 9
(0:17)

LITTLE BOXES

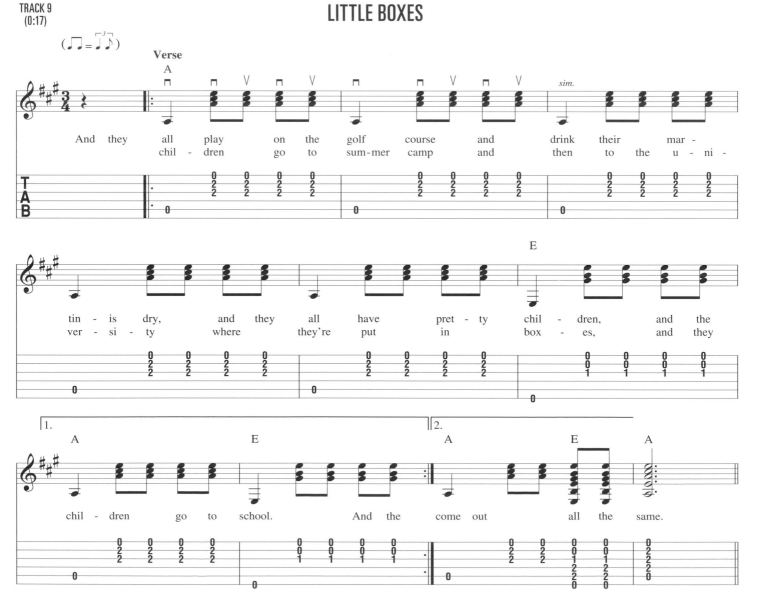

Words and Music by Malvina Reynolds
© Copyright 1962 SCHRODER MUSIC COMPANY (ASCAP)
Renewed 1990
All Rights Reserved   Used by Permission

FINGERPICKING

Fingerpicking means plucking the strings with your fingers, usually one string at a time. Sometimes two or more strings are plucked simultaneously. Some people use their bare fingers, others use fingerpicks, and some use their fingernails (and let them grow out for that purpose). Many folk guitarists play one- or two-bar fingerpicking patterns for accompaniment.

An Easy Cut-Time Pattern

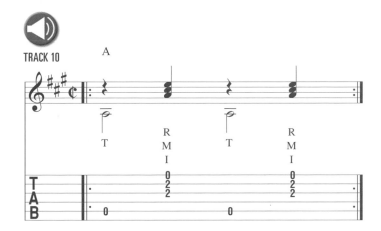

Here's a simple pattern that's useful for fast tempo "cut-time" tunes like the Appalachian version of "Tom Dooley."

1. The thumb picks a bass note, usually the root.

2. The index, middle, and ring fingers pick the third, second, and first strings simultaneously.

Here's a verse of "Tom Dooley" using this pattern.

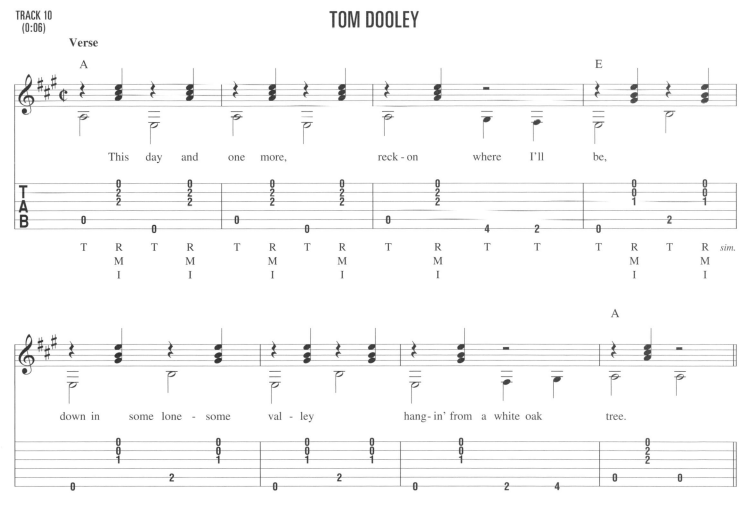

TOM DOOLEY

TRACK 10
(0:06)

Words and Music Collected, Adapted and Arranged by Frank Warner, John A. Lomax and Alan Lomax
From the singing of Frank Proffitt
TRO - © Copyright 1947 (Renewed) and 1958 (Renewed) Ludlow Music, Inc., New York, NY
International Copyright Secured
All Rights Reserved Including Public Performance For Profit
Used by Permission

Fingerpicking Pattern for Ballads

This fingerpicking pattern is more elaborate. If you listen to Track 11, you'll hear how the same pattern can be used to create a slow, country-style shuffle beat or a straight-eighth feel.

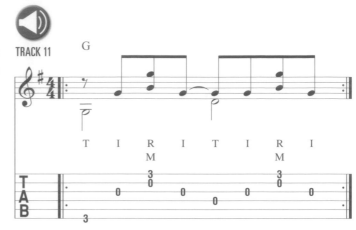

1. The thumb picks a bass note, usually the root.

2. The index finger picks the third string.

3. The middle and ring fingers pick the second and first strings, simultaneously.

4. And again, the index finger picks the third string.

5. Repeat the four steps starting with a different bass note.

This is a good accompaniment pattern for a ballad like "Suzanne," written by Canadian poet/singer-songwriter Leonard Cohen. Judy Collins' 1965 recording of the song made it very popular, and since then, it has been covered by singers as diverse as Harry Belafonte, Neil Diamond, Tori Amos, and Peter Gabriel.

TRACK 11
(0:09)

SUZANNE

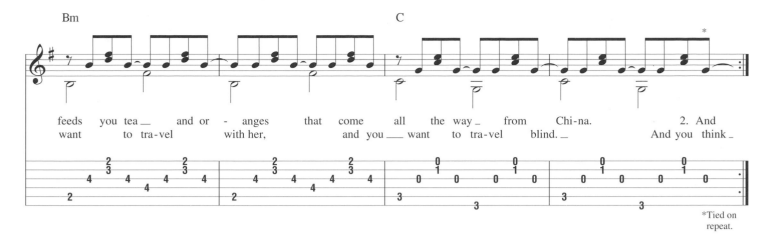

feeds you tea __ and or - anges that come all the way __ from Chi-na. 2. And
want to tra-vel with her, and you __ want to tra-vel blind. __ And you think __

*Tied on
repeat.

__ may-be __ you'll trust __ her, for she's touched your per - fect bod-y with her

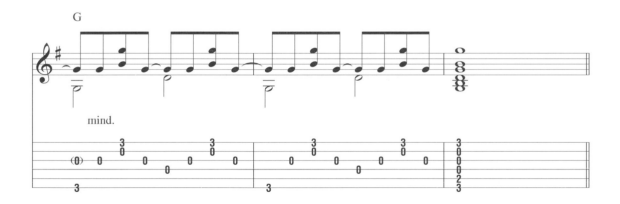

mind.

Additional Lyrics

3. And Jesus was a sailor when He walked upon the water,
    And He spent a long time watching from His lonely wooden tower.
    And when He knew for certain only drowning men could see Him,
    He said, "All men will be sailors then until the sea shall free them."
    But He Himself was broken long before the sky would open.
    Forsaken, almost human, He sank beneath your wisdom like a stone.
    And you want to travel with Him and you want to travel blind,
    And you think maybe you'll trust Him for He's touched your perfect body with His mind.

4. Now Suzanne takes your hand, and she leads you to the river.
    She is wearing rags and feathers from Salvation Army counters,
    And the sun pours down like honey on our lady of the harbour,
    And she shows you where to look among the garbage and the flowers.
    There are heroes in the seaweed; there are children in the morning.
    They are leaning out for love and they will lean that way forever,
    While Suzanne holds the mirror.
    And you want to travel with her, and you want to travel blind.
    And you know that you can trust her, for she's touched your perfect body with her mind.

Fingerpicking Waltz Pattern

The ballad fingerpicking pattern you just played has four steps: thumb, index, middle and ring, index. You can adapt it to 3/4 time by repeating the last two steps.

1. The thumb picks a bass note, usually the root.

2. The index finger picks the third string.

3. The middle and ring fingers pick the second and first strings, simultaneously.

4. The index finger picks the third string.

5. Again, the middle and ring fingers pick the second and first strings, simultaneously.

6. Finally, the index finger picks the third string once more.

The following version of "Scarborough Fair" shows how to use this pattern. Most people know the tune from Simon and Garfunkel's 1966 version, which became a pop hit when it was used in the film *The Graduate*. It's a traditional, centuries-old English ballad, and it had already been well-covered in films and folk/commercial recordings before the Simon and Garfunkel version, notably by Peggy Seeger and Ewan MacColl in the late 1950s.

TRACK 12
(0:06)

SCARBOROUGH FAIR

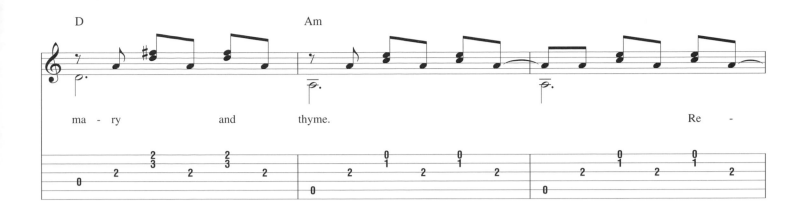

ma - ry   and   thyme.   Re -

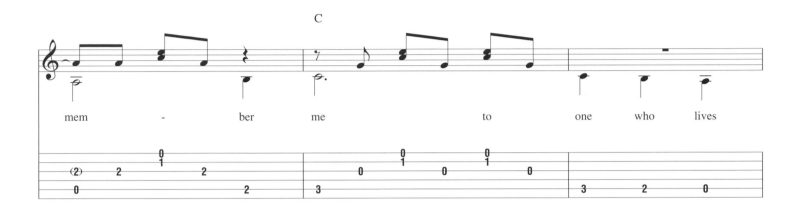

mem -   ber   me   to   one   who   lives

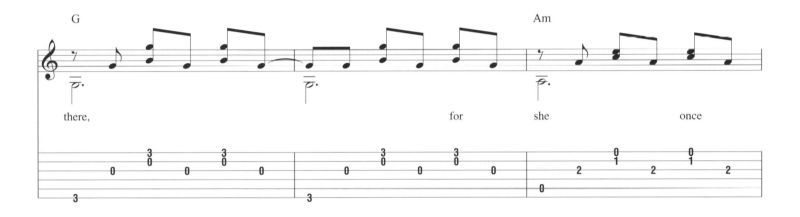

there,   for   she   once

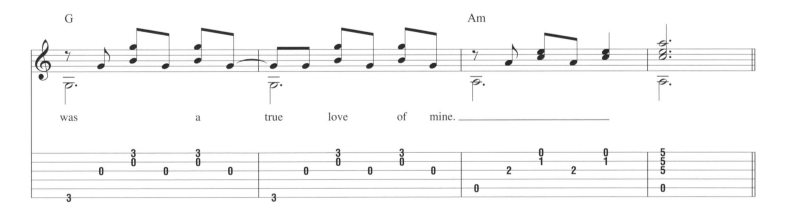

was   a   true   love   of   mine.

Additional Lyrics

2. Tell her to make me a cambric shirt. Parsley, sage, rosemary, and thyme.
   Without no seam or fine needlework. Then she'll be a true love of mine.

3. Tell her to find me an acre of land. Parsley, sage, rosemary, and thyme.
   Between the salt water and the sea strand. Then she'll be a true love of mine.

4. Tell her to reap it with a sickle of leather. Parsley, sage, rosemary, and thyme.
   And gather it all in a bunch of heather. Then she'll be a true love of mine.

6/8 Time Arpeggio Pattern

An *arpeggio* is a broken chord—i.e., the notes of a chord played one at a time in a sequence. An arpeggio can be played in any rhythm, and the notes can be played in any order. For example, an Am arpeggio could be played (among other ways) like this:

1. The thumb picks a bass note, usually the root.
2. The index finger picks the third string.
3. The middle finger picks the second string.
4. The ring finger picks the first string.
5. The middle finger picks the second string.
6. The index finger picks the third string.

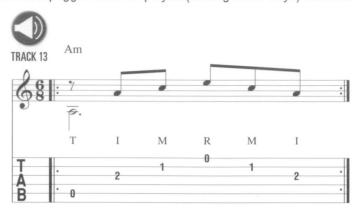

This arpeggio can also be played with a flatpick. Whichever way you play it, it works well as an accompaniment for "The House of the Rising Sun," a folk tune (about a brothel, a woman's prison, or something else) that became a pop hit when the rock group the Animals recorded it in 1964. The first recorded version was by North Carolina banjo/guitar picker Clarence Ashley in 1933, but the song may date back years further. It was recorded in the 1930s, 1940s, and 1950s by Roy Acuff, Woody Guthrie, Josh White, Leadbelly, the Weavers, and Frankie Laine; 1960s versions were also recorded by Joan Baez and Bob Dylan (again, on his first album in 1962)—the list goes on and on.

TRACK 13
(0:08)

THE HOUSE OF THE RISING SUN

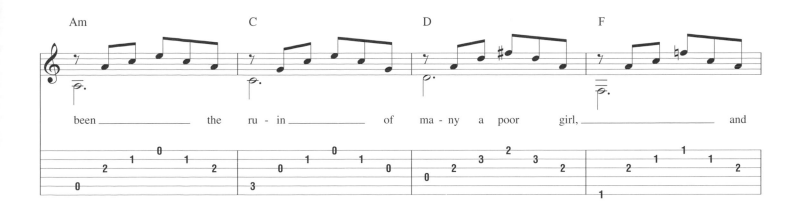

been _____ the ru - in _____ of ma - ny a poor girl, _____ and

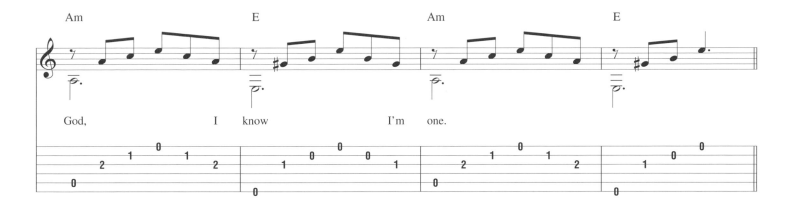

God, I know I'm one.

Additional Lyrics

2. My mother was a tailor; she sewed my old blue jeans.
   My father was a gambling man down in New Orleans.

3. The only thing a gambler needs is a suitcase and a trunk,
   And the only time he's satisfied is when he's on a drunk.

4. Go and tell my baby sister not to do what I have done,
   And shun that house in New Orleans that they call the Rising Sun.

5. I'm going back to New Orleans; my race is nearly run.
   I'm going to spend the rest of my life beneath the Rising Sun.

4/4 Time Arpeggio Pattern

There are countless arpeggio patterns to use in 4/4 time. Below is a popular one that is used to accompany "Where Have All the Flowers Gone?" (written by Pete Seeger in the 1950s), with some verses added a few years later by folksinger Joe Hickerson. This sad musical war story has also been covered by many artists of various genres in over twenty languages (including Chinese, Estonian, and Slovenian)!

For a G chord:

1. The thumb picks the sixth string (the root bass note).

2. The index finger picks the second string.

3. The middle finger picks the first string.

4. The thumb picks the fifth string.

5. The index finger picks the second string.

6. The middle finger picks the first string.

7. The thumb picks the fourth string.

8. The index finger picks the second string.

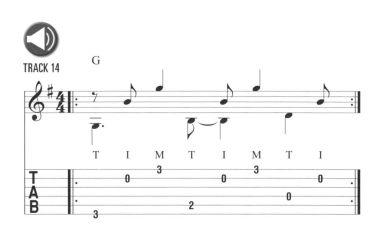

TRACK 14

WHERE HAVE ALL THE FLOWERS GONE?

Verse

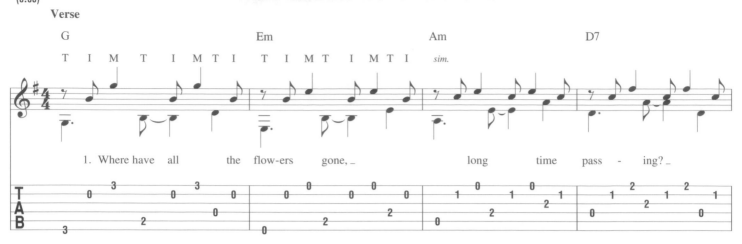

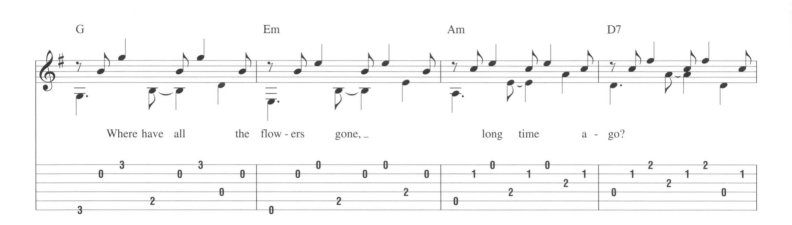

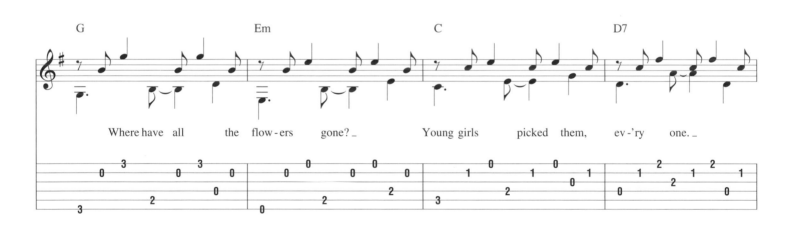

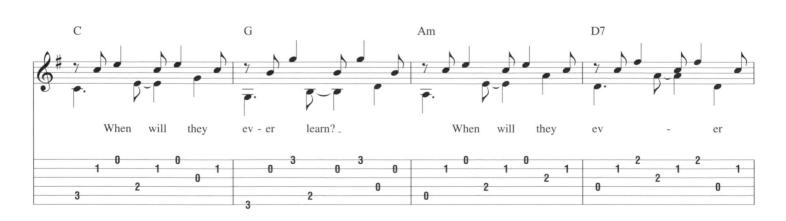

Words and Music by Pete Seeger
Copyright © 1961 (Renewed) by Sanga Music, Inc.
All Rights Reserved   Used by Permission

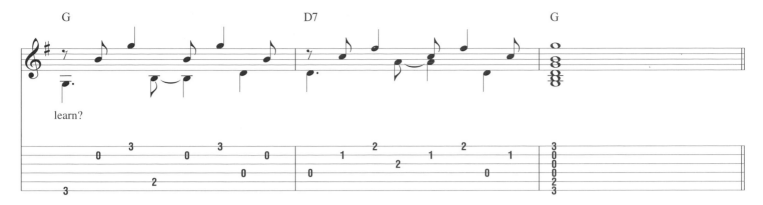

learn?

Additional Lyrics

2. Where have all the young girls gone, long time passing?
   Where have all the young girls gone, long time ago?
   Where have all the young girls gone? Taken husbands every one.
   When will they ever learn? When will they ever learn?

3. Where have all the young men gone, long time passing?
   Where have all the young men gone, long time ago?
   Where have all the young men gone? Gone for soldiers every one.
   When will they ever learn? When will they ever learn?

4. Where have all the soldiers gone, long time passing?
   Where have all the soldiers gone, long time ago?
   Where have all the soldiers gone? Gone to graveyards every one.
   When will they ever learn? When will they ever learn?

5. Where have all the graveyards gone, long time passing?
   Where have all the graveyards gone, long time ago?
   Where have all the graveyards gone? Gone to flowers every one.
   When will we ever learn? When will we ever learn?

The Basic Alternating-Thumb Blues Pattern

On many of the oldest recordings of blues guitarists from the 1920s and 1930s, the only repeated pattern is an alternating-thumb bass, playing on all four beats of a bar of 4/4 time.

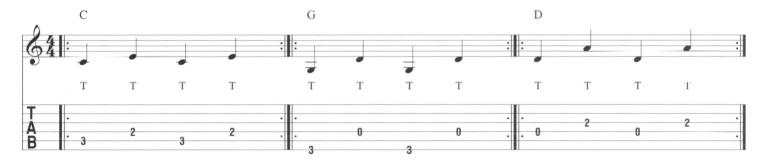

The genre is often called "raggy blues," referring to the bouncy ragtime beat generated by the alternating-thumb bass notes. Some trailblazing blues practitioners of the style included Mississippi John Hurt, Blind Blake, and "Blind" Willie McTell. Folk, country, blues, and rock guitarists have adapted this thumb pattern, adding other notes with the fingers.

Here's a basic, simple accompaniment pattern from which countless variations can be spun.

For a C chord:

1. The thumb picks the fifth string (the root bass note).

2. The index finger picks the second string.

3. The thumb picks the fourth string.

4. The middle finger picks the first string.

Many fingerpickers who use alternating-thumb patterns anchor their ring and little fingers on the guitar soundboard, just below the sound hole.

Here's how the basic alternating-thumb pattern sounds as accompaniment to the John Denver song, "Leaving on a Jet Plane." Denver wrote it in 1966, and many folk artists recorded it before Peter Paul & Mary made it a #1 pop hit in 1969.

TRACK 15
(0:11)

LEAVING ON A JET PLANE

Additional Lyrics

3. There's so many times I've let you down, so many times I've played around.
   I tell you now they don't mean a thing.

4. Ev'ry place I go I'll think of you; ev'ry song I sing, I sing for you.
   When I come back, I'll bring your wedding ring. *(Chorus)*

5. Now the time has come to leave you. One more time, let me kiss you,
   Then close your eyes; I'll be on my way.

6. Dream about the days to come when I won't have to leave alone,
   About the times I won't have to say: *(Chorus)*

Another Alternating-Thumb Pattern

The following version of "Puff the Magic Dragon" employs one of the many possible variations of the basic alternating-thumb pattern. The lick, used throughout the tune, starts with two octave notes: on a G chord, the thumb and middle finger play the sixth and first strings simultaneously. The thumb alternates between the sixth and third, rather than sixth and fourth strings.

For a G chord:

1. The thumb picks the sixth string while the middle finger picks the first string.

2. The thumb picks the third string.

3. The index finger picks the second string.

4. The thumb picks the sixth string.

5. The middle finger picks the first string.

6. The thumb picks the third string.

Use this pattern on the following backup part for "Puff the Magic Dragon." This song was written by Peter Yarrow (of Peter Paul & Mary) and a college roommate before Peter Paul & Mary existed as a formal group. The folk trio's recording of the song was a #2 pop hit in 1962 and has been made into a TV special and a book. It was intended to be and remains a classic children's song, and both Yarrow and Paul Stookey (also of Peter Paul & Mary) have always denied that this story about the loss of childish innocence has anything to do with marijuana, despite persistent, popular rumors.

TRACK 16
(0:09)

PUFF THE MAGIC DRAGON

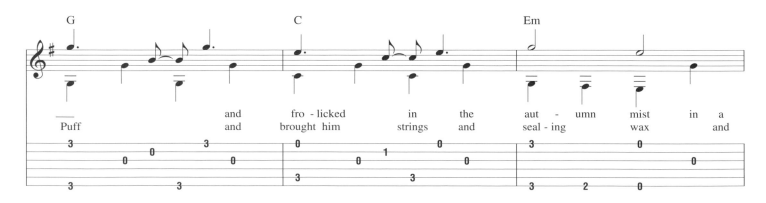

Words and Music by Lenny Lipton and Peter Yarrow
Copyright © 1963; Renewed 1991 Honalee Melodies (ASCAP) and Silver Dawn Music (ASCAP)
Worldwide Rights for Honalee Melodies Administered by BMG Rights Management (US) LLC
Worldwide Rights for Silver Dawn Music Administered by WB Music Corp.
International Copyright Secured   All Rights Reserved

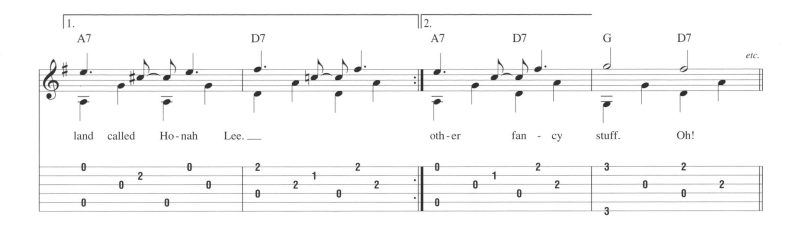

land called Ho-nah Lee. ___ oth-er fan-cy stuff. Oh!

Additional Lyrics

Chorus: Puff the magic dragon, lived by the sea
And frolicked in the autumn mist in a land called Honah Lee.
Puff the magic dragon, lived by the sea
And frolicked in the autumn mist in a land called Honah Lee.

2. Together they would travel on a boat with billowed sail. Jackie kept a lookout perched on Puff's gigantic tail.
Noble kings and princes would bow whene'er they came.
Pirate ships would lower their flags when Puff roared out his name. *(Chorus)*

3. A dragon lives forever but not so little boys. Painted wings and giant rings make way for other toys.
One grey night it happened, Jackie Paper came no more,
And Puff that mighty dragon, he ceased his fearless roar. *(Chorus)*

4. His head was bent in sorrow; green scales fell like rain. Puff no longer went to play along the cherry lane.
Without his life-long friend, Puff could not be brave,
So Puff that mighty dragon sadly slipped into his cave. *(Chorus)*

Two-Bar Alternating-Thumb Pattern

The following arrangement of Bob Dylan's "Don't Think Twice, It's All Right" shows how to craft a two-bar variation of the basic alternating-thumb pattern. This is a simplification of what Dylan actually played on his 1963 recording, *The Freewheelin'* *Bob Dylan* (second album). As in the sample two bars (below), he stayed off the first string most of the time, moving the pattern over a string so that the middle finger played the second string. He also did some "double alternating," as the thumb sometimes played the fifth string, fourth string, sixth string, and fourth string.

TRACK 17

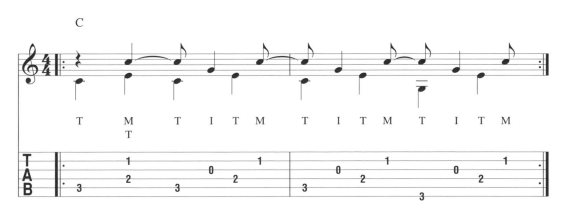

When it was released, the song struck a nerve—nearly every acoustic guitarist was playing it, and so was Johnny Cash, Elvis Presley, Doc Watson, Cher, Bobby Darin, Waylon Jennings, Flatt and Scruggs, and countless others. It remains an often-covered song through the decades with recent versions by Elliott Smith, Randy Travis, John Mayer, and Social Distortion.

DON'T THINK TWICE, IT'S ALL RIGHT

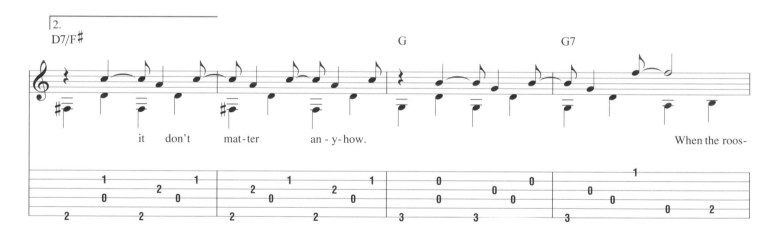

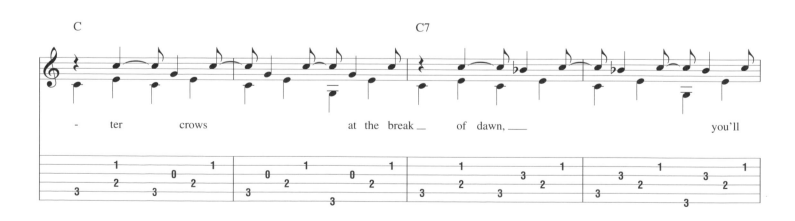

look out   your   win-dow   and   I'll   be __   gone. __

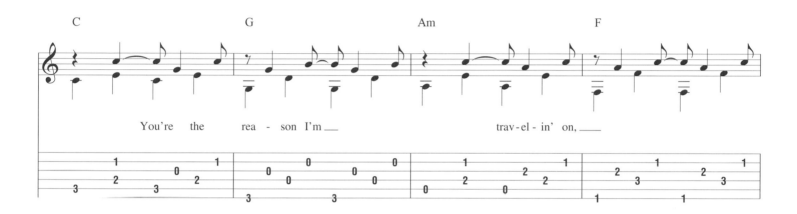

You're   the   rea - son   I'm __   trav-el-in'   on, __

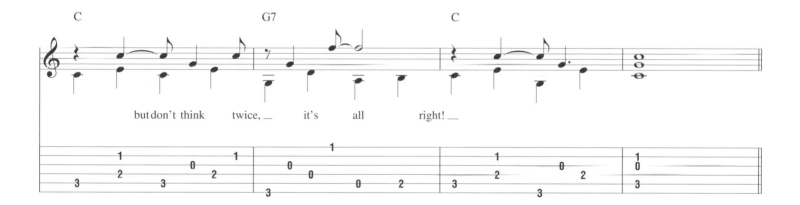

but don't think   twice, __   it's   all   right! __

Additional Lyrics

2. And it ain't no use turning on your light, babe, the light I never knowed.
   And it ain't no use turning on your light, babe. I'm on the dark side of the road.
   Still I wish there was something you could do or say to try to make me change my mind and stay.
   We never did much talking anyway, but don't think twice, it's all right.

3. I'm walkin' down this long lonesome road, babe. Where I'm bound I can't tell.
   But goodbye is too good of a word, babe, so I'll just say "fare thee well."
   I ain't sayin' that you treated me unkind. Could have done better, but I don't mind.
   You just sorta wasted my precious time, but don't think twice, it's all right.

4. And it ain't no use callin' out my name, babe, like you never did before.
   It ain't no use callin' out my name, babe. I can't hear you anymore.
   I'm a-thinkin' and a-wonderin' all the way down the road. I once loved a woman, a child I am told.
   I gave her my heart, but she wanted my soul. But don't think twice, it's all right.

SOLOING

Soloing means playing an instrumental break during a song. Most instrumental solos are melodic—you play the melody, a variation of it, or an ornamented melody. If you're unaccompanied (without a band to keep the momentum going), you'll need to support the melody with rhythmic chords by either strumming or fingerpicking. There are several ways to do this.

FLATPICKING

Flatpicking Solos – Carter Style

When Maybelle Carter played an instrumental solo, she usually picked the melody on the bass strings and used the Carter lick (brushing down on the treble strings) to keep the rhythm going. You have to finger the chord shapes while doing this, even though the melody may require you to add or take away a note from the normal chord.

The following arrangement of Woody Guthrie's anthemic "This Land Is Your Land" (written in 1940 and recorded a few years later) is a good example of this style. It was recorded by many well-known 1960s folksingers, and in later years, it has been covered by rockers, funk/soul bands, country musicians, and has become one of the most famous folk songs of all time—often taught in public schools all over the U.S.

TRACK 18

THIS LAND IS YOUR LAND—FLATPICKING SOLO

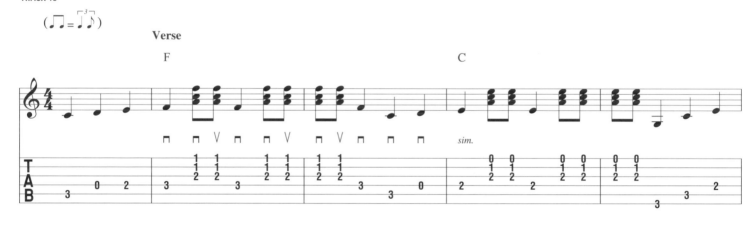

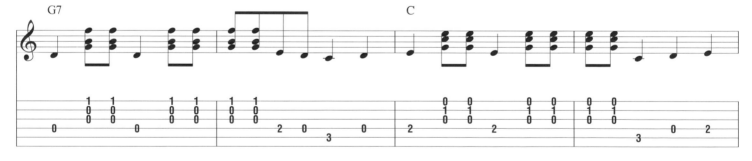

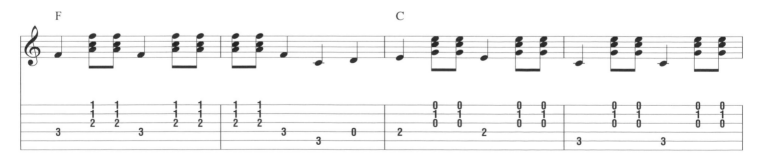

Words and Music by Woody Guthrie
TRO - © Copyright 1956 (Renewed), 1958 (Renewed), 1970 (Renewed) and 1972 (Renewed) Ludlow Music, Inc., New York, NY
International Copyright Secured
All Rights Reserved Including Public Performance For Profit
Used by Permission

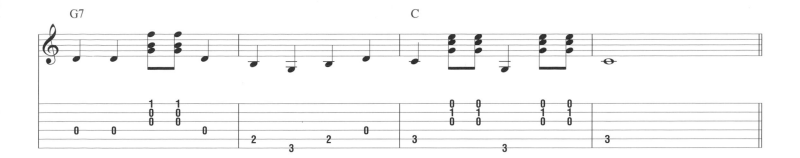

Lyrics

Chorus: This land is your land, this land is my land, from California to the New York Island.
From the Redwood Forest to the Gulf Stream waters, this land was made for you and me.

1. As I was walking a ribbon of highway, I saw above me an endless skyway.
I saw below me a golden valley. This land was made for you and me.

2. I've roamed and rambled and I've followed my footsteps
To the sparkling sands of her diamond deserts.
And all around me a voice was sounding, "This land was made for you and me."

3. The sun came shining as I was strolling,
The wheat fields waving and the dust clouds rolling.
As the fog was lifting, a voice come chanting, "This land was made for you and me."

4. As I was walkin', I saw a sign there, and that sign said "No tresspassin'!"
But on the other side, it didn't say nothin'! Now that side was made for you and me!

5. In the squares of the city, in the shadow of the steeple,
Near the relief office, I see my people.
And some are grumblin', and some are wonderin' if this land's still made for you and me.

Adding Hammer-Ons and Pull-Offs

Most flatpickers ornament melodies by adding hammer-ons and pull-offs. These are left-hand techniques in which you sound a note with your fret hand.

- *Hammering-on* means sounding a note by fretting it suddenly with a fretting finger. In tablature, a slur connecting two numbers indicates a hammer-on. Here are two examples. In the first, you pick the open third string and hammer on at the second fret—you should hear two distinct notes. In the second example, you pick the third string at the second fret and, using a different finger than the one that's already fretting the third string, hammer on to the third fret. Again, you should hear two distinct notes.

- *Pulling-off* means sounding a note by plucking down on a string with a fretting finger. In the first example, play the third string at the second fret and pluck down with your fretting finger to sound the open third string. In the second example, fret the third string at the second fret with your index finger and at the third fret with your middle finger. Pick the string and pluck down with your middle finger so that you hear two distinct notes.

The solo that follows is a lead break for the Graham Nash tune "Teach Your Children." The hammer-ons and pull-offs imitate the way the melody sounds when sung. The song was recorded on Crosby, Stills, Nash & Young's 1970 *Déjà Vu* album. Much of their music has a folky sound, and the pedal steel playing (supplied by Jerry Garcia!) gave this rendition a country flavor as well.

TRACK 19
(0:17)

TEACH YOUR CHILDREN—SOLO

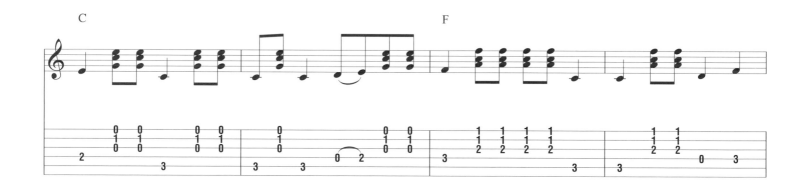

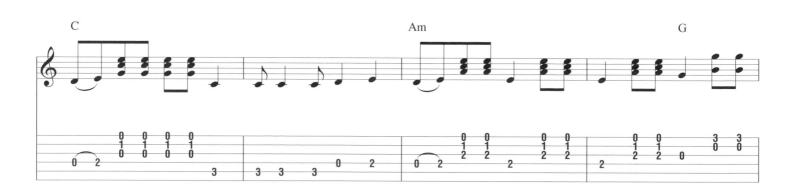

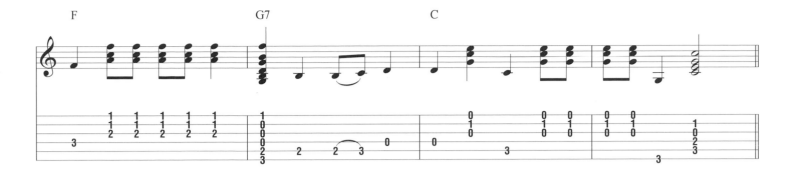

Lyrics

1. You who are on the road must have a code that you can live by,
   And so become yourself, because the past is just a goodbye.
   Teach your children well; their father's hell did slowly go by.
   And feed them on your dreams; the one they pick's the one you'll know by.
   Don't you ever ask them why; if they told you, you would cry,
   So just look at them and sigh and know they love you.

2. And you, of tender years, can't know the fears that your elders grew by.
   And so please help them with your youth; they seek the truth before they can die.
   Teach your parents well; their children's hell will slowly go by.
   And feed them on your dreams; the one they pick's the one you'll know by.
   Don't you ever ask them why; if they told you, you would cry,
   So just look at them and sigh and know they love you.

Flatpicking a Solo with Calypso Rhythm

The Carter-style method of playing the melody on the lower strings and strumming the higher strings for rhythm isn't just for country-style songs; it can be used with many different rhythmic grooves, such as the calypso groove of "Sloop John B." In the following flatpicking solo, "fill out" the melody by strumming through all the pauses in the melodic line.

SLOOP JOHN B.—SOLO

TRACK 20

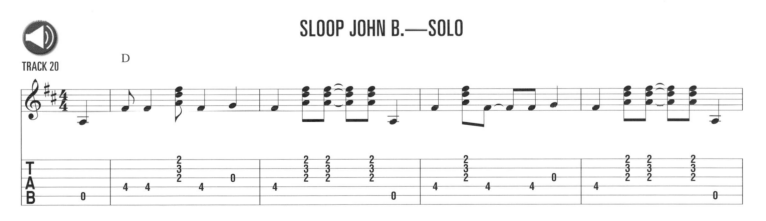

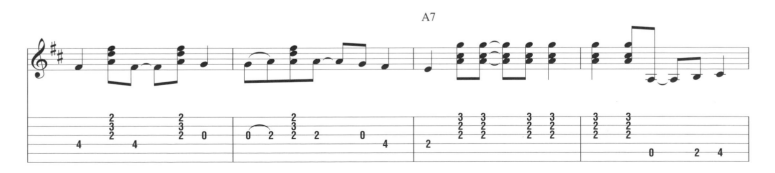

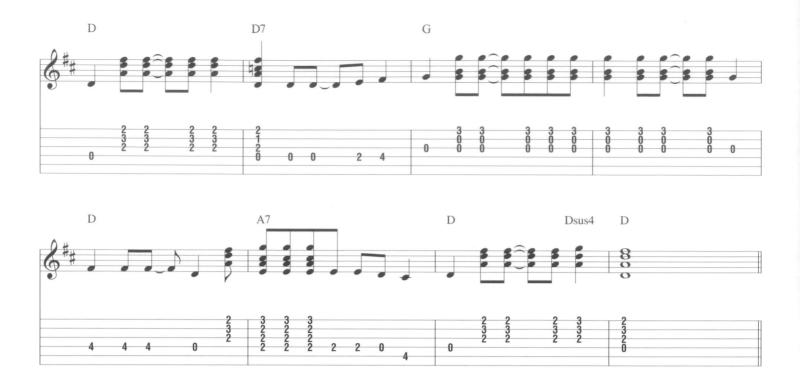

Flatpicking a Solo with Folk-Rock Rhythm

The next solo has a straight-eighth rock feel. Once again, the melody is filled out with downstrokes and upstrokes on the treble strings. "Guantanamera" was a popular Cuban song in the late 1920s, and several decades later, Spanish composer Julian Orbon adapted a poem by Cuban hero/philosopher/freedom fighter José Marti to the popular melody. In the early 1960s, Pete Seeger popularized this version, which was practically the Cuban national anthem. It has since been performed by folkies like Arlo Guthrie and Joan Baez, as well as pop stars Trini Lopez, the folk group the Sandpipers, José Feliciano, Jimmy Buffett, the Fugees, Wyclef Jean, and many more Cuban singers.

GUANTANAMERA—SOLO

TRACK 21

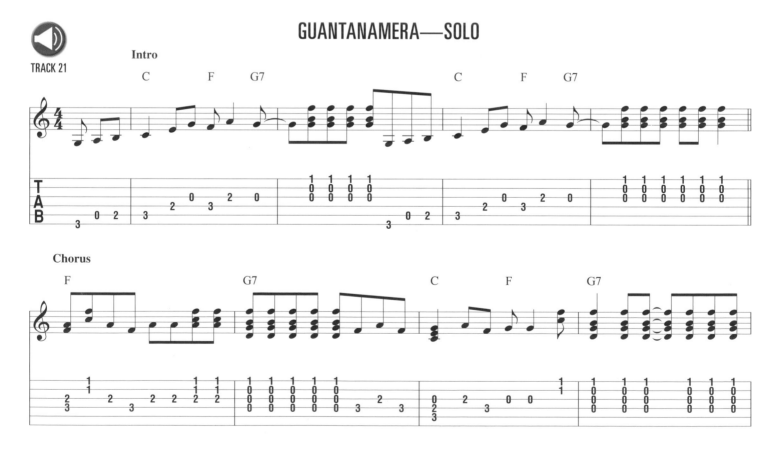

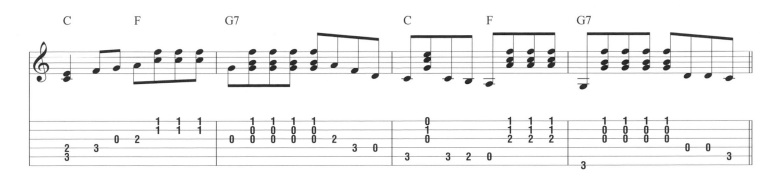

Verse

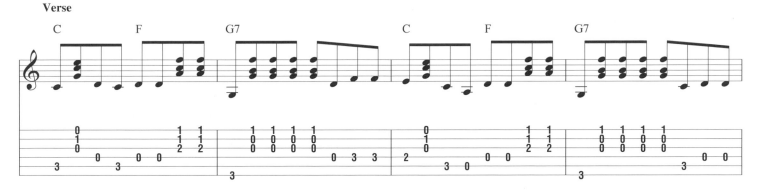

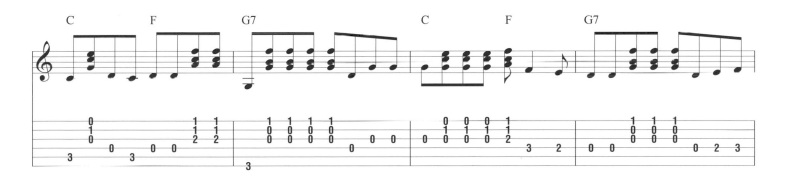

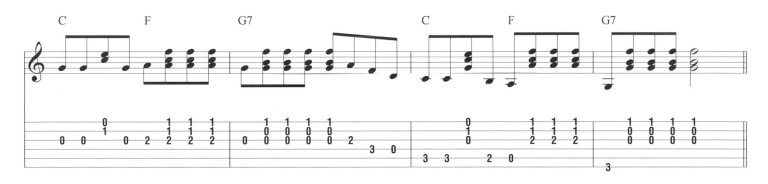

Lyrics

Chorus: Guantanamera, guajira Guantanamera, Guantanamera, guajira Guantanamera.

1. Yo soy un hombre sincero de donde crecen las palmas.
   Yo soy un hombre sincero de donde crecen las palmas.
   Y antes de morirme quiero echar mis versos del alma.

   (A truthful man, that's me, from where the palm trees grow.
   Before dying, I should like to pour forth the poems of my soul.)

2. Mi verso es de un verde claro y de un carmin encendido.
   Mi verso es de un verde claro y de un carmin encendido.
   Mi verso es un ciervo herido que busca en el monte amparo.

   (My verses are of soft green, but also a flowing red.
   My verse is a wounded faun seeking refuge in the woods.)

3. Con los pobres de la tierra quiero yo mi suerte echar.
   Con los pobres de la tierra quiero yo mi suerte echar.
   El arroyo de la sierra me complace mas que el mar.

   (With the humble of the earth, my fate I want to share,
   For the gentle stream of a mountain pleases me more than the sea.)

Flatpicking a Solo in 3/4 Time

The Carter style works well for solos in waltz time. Let's revisit "Little Boxes" with a Carter-style solo.

TRACK 22

LITTLE BOXES—FLATPICKING SOLO

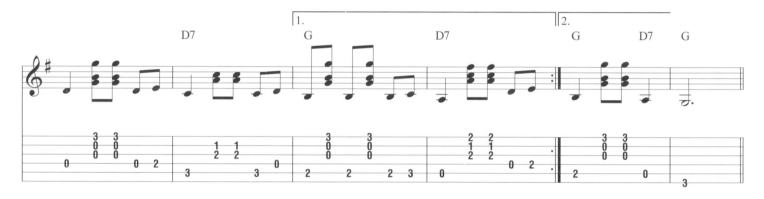

FINGERPICKING

Fingerpicking a Solo with Alternating-Thumb Bass

When Greenwich Village (Manhattan) was a hotbed of aspiring young folksingers at the beginning of the 1960s, Tom Paxton, Bob Dylan, and Phil Ochs would sit together in a café studying Mississippi John Hurt as he fingerpicked "My Creole Belle," "Candy Man," and hundreds of other tunes; they adapted his alternating-thumb bass style to their songs. Additionally, folkies everywhere listened to and learned to imitate the licks of blues fingerpickers like John Hurt.

It sounds simple: keep that alternating-thumb bass going (playing all four downbeats of each bar) while you play the melody with your fingers on the treble strings. The catch is that many people find their thumb bass drags along with the melody notes and gets off track. If this happens to you, try learning the melody first, then add the bass (if necessary), repeating one bar at a time and learning the song bar by bar. It pays off, as the second song comes much easier than the first.

Here's a simple instrumental solo for "This Land Is Your Land," played in the alternating-thumb bass style.

THIS LAND IS YOUR LAND—FINGERPICKING SOLO

Fingerpicking a Solo with Syncopation

In the previous solo for "This Land Is Your Land," all of the melody notes coincide with thumb bass notes. If you occasionally slip a melody note *between* the thumb bass notes, you get a more syncopated sound. The resulting solo usually sounds more like the song's actual melody, because most tunes include some syncopation.

The following solo for Dylan's "Blowin' in the Wind" includes several "between-the-bass" melody notes. When it was written in 1962, the song was a major breakthrough for Dylan and all his folk-singing peers. Along with "A Hard Rain's A-Gonna Fall," it raised the bar—lyrically—for songwriters everywhere. A few months after it appeared on Dylan's second album (1963's *The Freewheelin' Bob Dylan*), Peter Paul & Mary's version of the song became a huge pop hit. It has been recorded by hundreds of artists in many languages and is forever linked with protests, the civil rights movement, and progressive causes. Dylan later acknowledged that the song is his adaptation of "No More Auction Block for Me"—an old spiritual that was sung by former slaves.

BLOWIN' IN THE WIND—FINGERPICKING SOLO

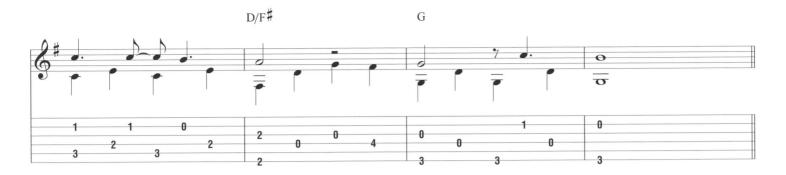

Lyrics

1. How many roads must a man walk down before they call him a man?
   How many seas must a white dove sail before she sleeps in the sand?
   How many times must the cannonballs fly before they are forever banned?
   The answer, my friend, is blowin' in the wind; the answer is blowin' in the wind.

2. How many years can a mountain exist before it is washed to the sea?
   How many years can some people exist before they're allowed to be free?
   Yes, and how many times can a man turn his head and pretend that he just doesn't see?
   The answer, my friend, is blowin' in the wind; the answer is blowin' in the wind.

3. How many times must a man look up before he can see the sky?
   How many ears must one man have before he can hear people cry?
   Yes, and how many deaths will it take 'til he knows that too many people have died?
   The answer, my friend, is blowin' in the wind; the answer is blowin' in the wind.

Fingerpicking a Solo with a Pattern

Some fingerpickers use a one- or two-bar pattern (like the patterns described in the Accompaniment section of this book) for soloing. Usually, this involves some occasional variation of the pattern to make the melody happen. For example, the pattern written below is sometimes used in playing Elizabeth Cotten's "Freight Train":

TRACK 25

Elizabeth "Libba" Cotten grew up in North Carolina and wrote "Freight Train" when she was a teenager. Later in life, the Seeger family employed her as a housekeeper in Washington D.C. and discovered that she sang and fingerpicked the guitar "upside down" (she was left-handed, but did not re-string the right-handed guitar). Mike Seeger helped get her started performing, recording, and touring on the folk and blues circuits, and she continued to do so well into her eighties. Budding fingerpickers used to be required to learn "Freight Train" and other Cotten compositions; as a result, her songs have become often-recorded folk favorites.

FREIGHT TRAIN—SOLO

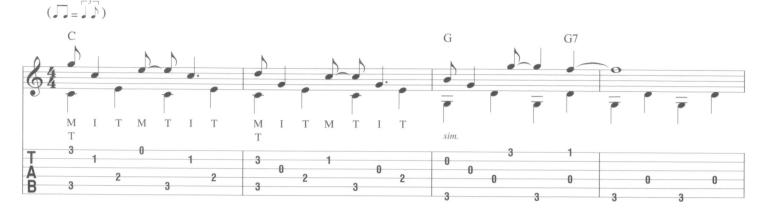

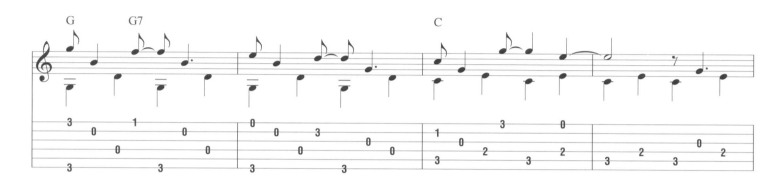

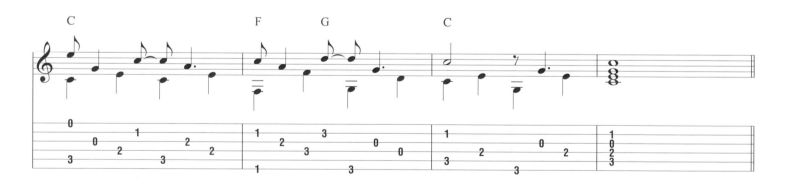

Lyrics

1. Freight train, freight train, run so fast; freight train, freight train, run so fast.
   Please don't tell them what train I'm on so they won't know what route I've gone.

2. When I am dead and in my grave, no more good time here I crave.
   Place the stones at my head and feet and tell them all that I've gone to sleep.

3. When I die, Lord, bury me deep way down on old Chestnut Street
   So I can hear old Number Nine as she goes rolling by.

Fingerpicking a Solo with a Different Pattern

Here's a variant of the "Freight Train" fingerpicking pattern:

TRACK 26

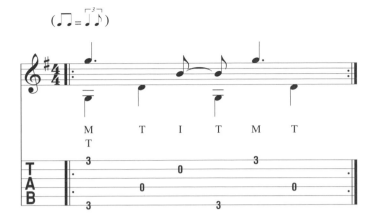

And here's a solo for "Puff the Magic Dragon," based on the above pattern.

TRACK 26
(0:07)

PUFF THE MAGIC DRAGON—SOLO

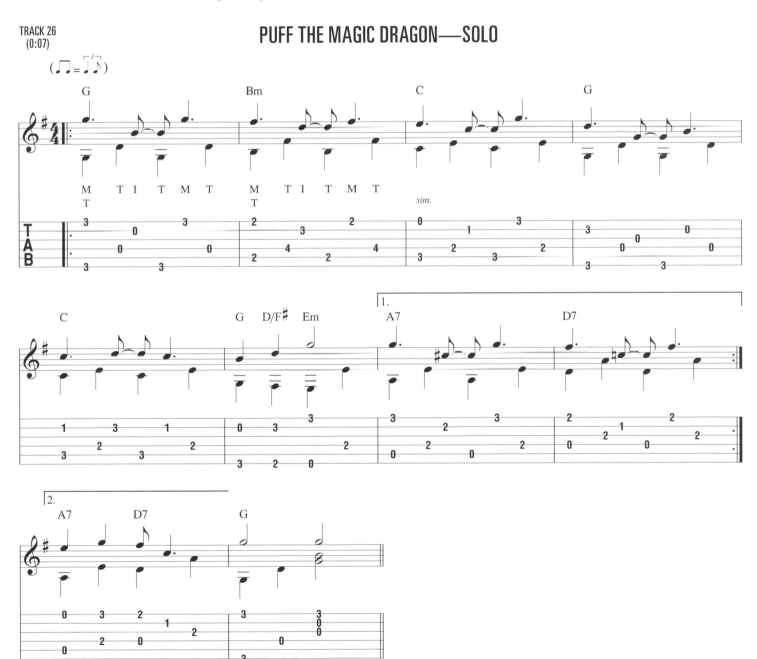

Fingerpicking a Solo with Embellishments

The following solo for "Don't Think Twice, It's All Right" has an alternating-thumb bass and an approximation of the melody played on the treble strings (just like the solo version of "This Land Is Your Land"). However, it also includes several embellishments: hammer-ons, bass runs, and pull-offs. To make it sound even more like the original album version, capo up four frets and play it *fast*!

DON'T THINK TWICE, IT'S ALL RIGHT—SOLO

TRACK 27

Fingerpicking a Solo with a Folk-Rock Rhythm

The solo for "Turn! Turn! Turn! (To Everything There Is a Season)" sometimes diverges from the steady, alternating-thumb bass, but the rhythm never lets up. It shows how you can occasionally alter the bass pattern to accommodate the melody and create some rhythmic variation. Pete Seeger wrote the tune in 1959, adapting prose from the Bible's *Book of Ecclesiastes*. It was first recorded in 1962 by the folk trio, the Limeliters, and in 1965, the Byrds electrified it and made it a #1 pop hit. It also charted in Europe. This song has been covered by many artists.

TURN! TURN! TURN! (TO EVERYTHING THERE IS A SEASON)—SOLO

TRACK 28

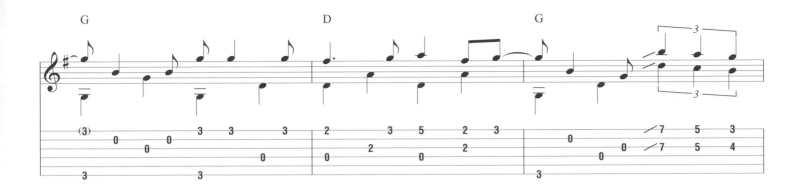

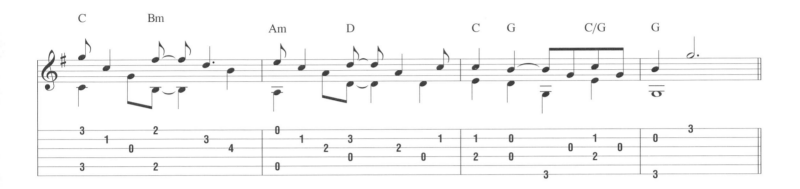

Lyrics

1. To everything (turn, turn, turn), there is a season (turn, turn, turn)
   And a time to every purpose under heaven.
   A time to be born, a time to die, a time to plant, a time to reap,
   A time to kill, a time to heal, a time to laugh, a time to weep.

2. To everything (turn, turn, turn), there is a season (turn, turn, turn)
   And a time to every purpose under heaven.
   A time to build up, a time to break down, a time to dance, a time to mourn,
   A time to cast away stones, a time to gather stones together.

3. To everything (turn, turn, turn), there is a season (turn, turn, turn)
   And a time to every purpose under heaven.
   A time of love, a time of hate, a time of war, a time of peace,
   A time you may embrace, a time to refrain from embracing.

4. To everything (turn, turn, turn), there is a season (turn, turn, turn)
   And a time to every purpose under heaven.
   A time to gain, a time to lose, a time to rend, a time to sew,
   A time for love, a time for hate, a time for peace, I swear it's not too late.

Fingerpicking a Solo with Arpeggios

In Carter-style flatpicking, brush strokes on the treble strings fill out the spaces between melody notes and keep the rhythm going. Fingerpickers sometimes use a different approach: playing the melody wherever you find it (in the bass strings or the treble strings) and playing arpeggios to fill out the rhythm.

In the following solo for "Greenfields," the thumb picks most of the melody on the bass strings. The highest melody notes are played on the treble strings and picked by the fingers. The spaces between melody notes are "filled" with arpeggios that ascend (if the melody is on low strings) or descend (if the melody is on high strings).

GREENFIELDS—SOLO

TRACK 29

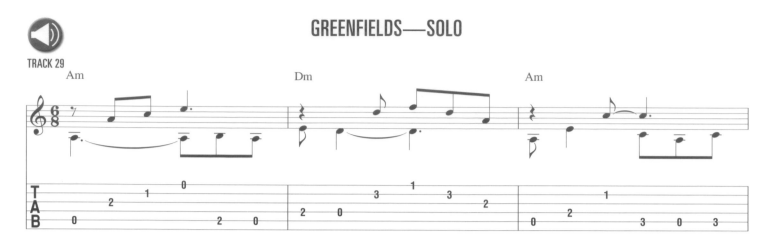

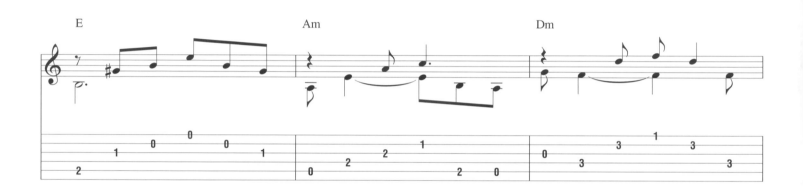

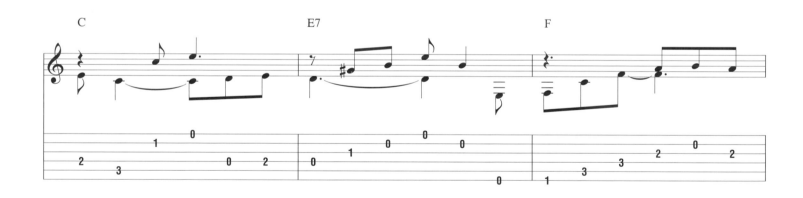

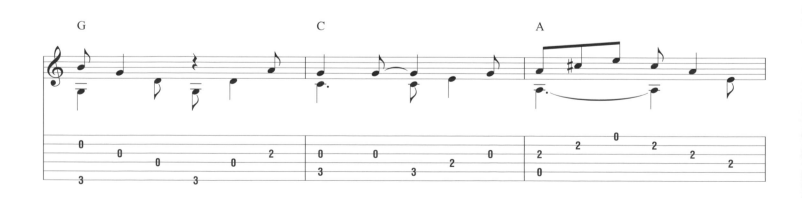

Words and Music by Terry Gilkyson, Richard Dehr and Frank Miller
© 1956, 1960 (Renewed 1984, 1988) EMI BLACKWOOD MUSIC INC.
All Rights Reserved   International Copyright Secured   Used by Permission

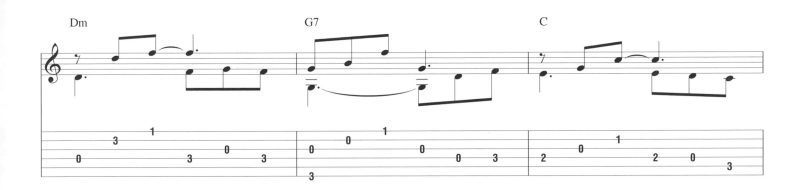

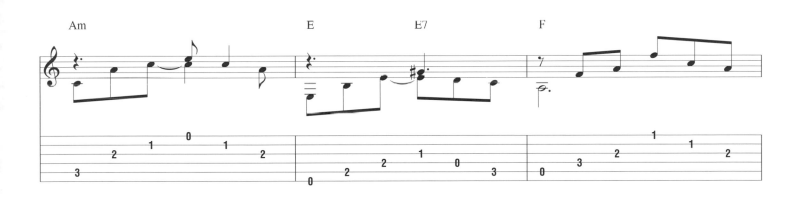

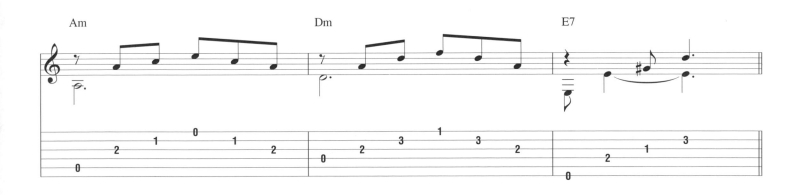

THE I–IV–V CHORD FAMILY

A little bit of music theory can make you a more well-rounded player. It can help you understand how to play a song in any key (so you can match the tune to your vocal range), and it can help you communicate with other players. Understanding music theory can also make it easier to learn new songs. What follows is one aspect of music theory—a simple concept that is especially helpful in playing folk music: the I–IV–V chord family.

Folk tunes tend to have simple chord progressions; they often consist of just three chords: the I, IV, and V chords (pronounced, "the one, four, and five chords"). What do these Roman numerals mean? So far in this book, only letters like C and G have been used to describe chords. These numbers relate to *degrees*, or notes, in the major scale.

C is the first note in the C major scale, so if a song is in the key of C, C is called the "I chord." D is the second note of the C major scale, so in the key of C, a D, Dm, or D7 chord is called the "II chord." E is called the "III chord," and so on.

Whatever key you're in, I, IV, and V are closely related: they're often referred to as a "chord family." In the key of C, C is the I chord, F is the IV chord, and G (the fifth note in the C major scale) is the V chord. C, F, and G are the *C chord family*, and millions of songs can be played in the key of C with these three chords.

I, IV, and V chord changes have recognizable sounds. Eventually, just by listening, you will know when a song goes from I to V, or I to IV—regardless of key. One way to develop your ear's ability to recognize these sounds is to play a song that goes from I to IV to V—over and over—in several keys. Check out the following Chord Family Chart:

Chord Family Chart

I	IV	V
C	F	G
G	C	D
D	G	A
A	D	E
E	A	B

As an example, strum the following arrangement of "I Am a Man of Constant Sorrow," playing along with Track 30. Each verse is in a different key: The first verse is in C, the second is in G, the third is in D, the fourth is in A, and the fifth is in E. Realize, as you play the tune, that the beginning chord of each verse is the I chord; the first change is to the IV chord, the next change is to the V, and then you return to the I. This sequence happens over and over in each verse. Use the Chord Family Chart (above) to find the IV and V chords in each key, then play along with the recording.

Song in Five Keys

I AM A MAN OF CONSTANT SORROW

TRACK 30

Here's another ear training exercise: play a steady strum, changing from the I chord to the IV chord in the five keys (from the Chord Family Chart) and listen for the similarity in sound. Then follow a similar pattern, but going from the I to the V chord.

Strumming from I to IV and I to V in Five Keys

TRACK 31

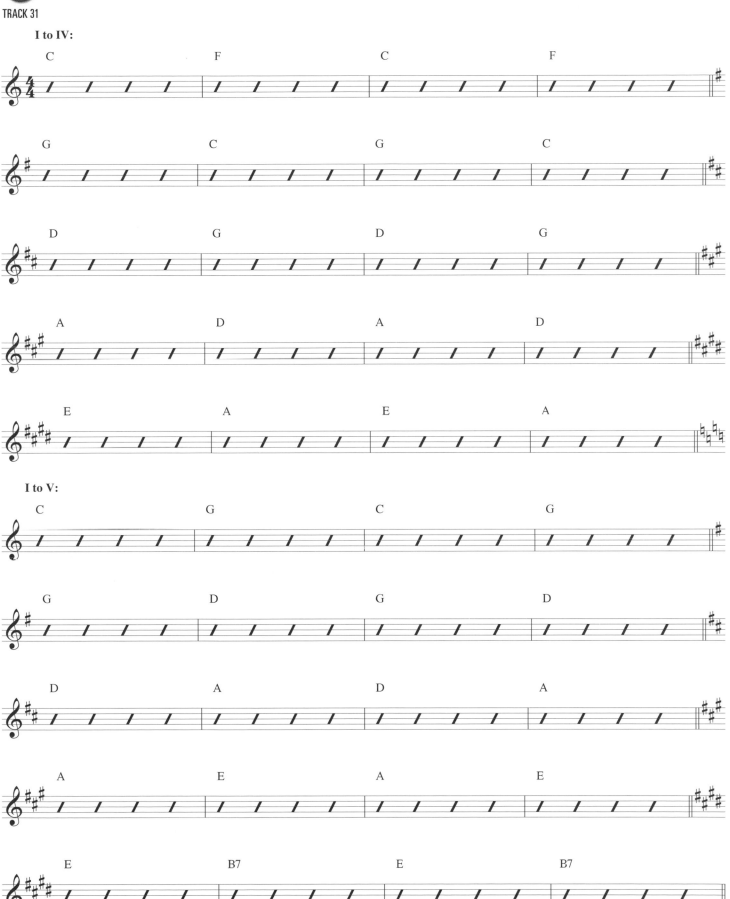

USING A CAPO

Any song can be played in any key. A singer's vocal range is usually the determining factor in choosing a key. So, the guitarist has to be prepared to play in any key—including guitar-unfriendly keys like B, F, and E♭. These keys normally require a lot of barred chords (the *barre* is the flattening of a finger across the fingerboard to fret multiple strings). However, a simple, inexpensive device called a *capo* enables you to "cheat" (capos used to be called "cheaters"); they enable you to use easy, first-position chords in any key.

Many capo shapes and styles can be found in music stores (see the photos below), but they all do the same thing.

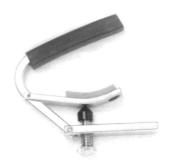

Shubb "Original" Capo

Kyser "Quick Change" Capo

Once you clamp the capo at, say, the second fret, it's as if the guitar begins at that fret. When you place your capo on fret 2, three things are immediately apparent:

- The first two frets are unusable.

- Every chord shape sounds two frets higher. Your G chord is now an A chord, your C chord sounds like D, and so on.

Best of all, the capo helps you play in difficult keys. The chart below shows how to use the capo to play in any key, using easy first-position chords. It offers choices for most keys. For example, to play in the key of B♭, you can capo at the first fret, and the first-position A chord then becomes a B♭ chord—or—you can capo at the third fret and play a first-position G chord, which then sounds like B♭.

CAPO CHART

To play in the key of	capo at fret #	and play a 1st position
A♭	1	G
	4	E
A	2	G
	5	E
B♭	1	A
	3	G
B	2	A
	4	G
C	3	A
	5	G
D♭	1	C
	4	A

To play in the key of	capo at fret #	and play a 1st position
D	2	C
E♭	1	D
	3	C
E	2	D
	4	C
F	1	E
	3	D
	5	C
G♭	2	E
	4	D
	6	C
G	3	E
	7	C

Once you have used the above Capo Chart to find your I chord, use the more complete Chord Family Chart below to find the IV and V chords:

COMPLETE I–IV–V CHORD FAMILY CHART

I chord	IV chord	V chord
A♭	D♭	E♭
A	D	E
B♭	E♭	F
B	E	F♯
C	F	G
D♭	G♭	A♭
D	G	A
E♭	A♭	B♭
E	A	B
F	B♭	C
G♭	C♭ (B)	D♭
G	C	D

Suppose you want to play "I Am a Man of Constant Sorrow" in the key of B, because it suits your vocal range. The Capo Chart says that if you capo at the fourth fret, the first-position G chord shape is your I chord (B). The Chord Family Chart says that C and D are the IV and V chords, respectively, that go with the G (I) chord. It also says that, since the capoed G chord is really a B, the IV and V chords are really E and F♯.

Experiment: Use the Capo Chart and Chord Family Chart to play other songs in this book in other keys.

WHERE TO GO FROM HERE

To learn more folk music and improve your playing:

Listen to performers who have contributed to and created the styles of music you like (see the "Listening Suggestions" chapter that follows) and listen to and go to see contemporary performers who have a lot to contribute, musically.

Learn from music books and instructional DVDs that teach songs, styles, and techniques relevant to folk music. The following Hal Leonard books (also written by Fred Sokolow) are recommended:

Basic Blues for Guitar

Basic Fingerpicking

Bluegrass Guitar Method

The Carter Family Collection

Fretboard Roadmaps - Bluegrass and Folk Guitar

Fretboard Roadmaps for Acoustic Guitar

Fretboard Roadmaps - Alternate Guitar Tunings

Fretboard Roadmaps - Slide Guitar

Gospel Guitar Songbook

The Jimmie Rodgers Collection

John Sebastian Songbook

The Hank Williams Songbook

Jam with other players and singers who like folk music. If they're not in your present circle of friends, they can be found in folk music clubs, online groups, and local music stores that are acoustically oriented. Playing music with other people helps you grow musically, and it can be a lot of fun.

Good Luck,

Fred Sokolow

Fred Sokolow

P.S. If you have any questions, contact me at www.sokolowmusic.com.

LISTENING SUGGESTIONS

Most of the songs in this book are from the folk boom of the late 1950s through the early 1960s—a brief period when folk music (somewhat polished for urban audiences) was accepted by a pop audience. Some of the main performers of that era were Pete Seeger (with and without the Weavers), the Kingston Trio, the Limeliters, Woody Guthrie, Joan Baez, Bob Dylan, Judy Collins, Odetta, Burl Ives, Tom Paxton, Josh White, and Peter Paul & Mary. These urban folksingers were influenced by blues, bluegrass, and old-time musicians (among other genres).

Some other folkies who are worth sampling (and possibly watching—on YouTube.com) include:

Blues: Mississippi John Hurt, Lightnin' Hopkins, Robert Johnson, "Blind" Willie McTell, Skip James, Brownie McGhee and Sonny Terry, Reverend Gary Davis, Mississippi Fred McDowell, Blind Blake, Mississippi Sheiks, Charlie Patton, Big Bill Broonzy, Bukka White, Furry Lewis, and Big Joe Williams (1 and 2).

Bluegrass: Pioneers include Bill Monroe & His Blue Grass Boys, Flatt and Scruggs and the Foggy Mountain Boys, the Stanley Brothers (and Ralph Stanley), Jimmy Martin, Jim and Jesse McReynolds, the Country Gentlemen, the Kentucky Colonels (with Clarence White), Reno & Smiley, the Greenbriar Boys, and Mac Wiseman.

A few contemporary bluegrassers include the Nashville Bluegrass Band, Del McCoury, Alison Krauss, Laurie Lewis, Rhonda Vincent, the Punch Brothers, and Alison Brown.

Old-Time (string band music that pre-dates bluegrass): the Carter Family, Jimmie Rodgers, Doc Watson, Charlie Poole, Charlie Monroe, Clarence Ashley, the New Lost City Ramblers, Uncle Dave Macon, Bascom Lunsford, Dock Boggs, J.E. Mainer's Mountaineers, Gid Tanner & His Skillet Lickers, McGee Brothers, Roscoe Holcomb, the Red Clay Ramblers, and Highwoods String Band (the last two are early 1970s revival bands who performed and recorded old-time music).

There's a new wave of old-time performers, some very traditional, like the Carolina Chocolate Drops, Frank Fairfield and Blind Boy Paxton; others in the new bluegrass/old-time/jam band genre include Old Crow Medicine Show, the Avett Brothers, Fleet Foxes, and Mumford & Sons.

Listen to the newly-released *Harry Smith's Anthology of American Folk Music*, originally released in 1952, which so inspired the folkies of the late '50s and early '60s. This extensive collection of old-time and blues music continues to inspire players of all genres.

GUITAR NOTATION LEGEND

Guitar music can be notated three different ways: on a *musical staff*, in *tablature*, and in *rhythm slashes*.

RHYTHM SLASHES are written above the staff. Strum chords in the rhythm indicated. Use the chord diagrams found at the top of the first page of the transcription for the appropriate chord voicings. Round noteheads indicate single notes.

THE MUSICAL STAFF shows pitches and rhythms and is divided by bar lines into measures. Pitches are named after the first seven letters of the alphabet.

TABLATURE graphically represents the guitar fingerboard. Each horizontal line represents a string, and each number represents a fret.

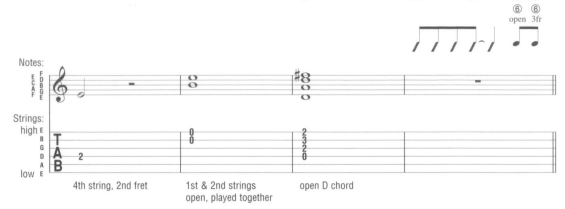

4th string, 2nd fret   1st & 2nd strings open, played together   open D chord

DEFINITIONS FOR SPECIAL GUITAR NOTATION

HALF-STEP BEND: Strike the note and bend up 1/2 step.

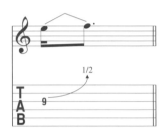

WHOLE-STEP BEND: Strike the note and bend up one step.

GRACE NOTE BEND: Strike the note and immediately bend up as indicated.

SLIGHT (MICROTONE) BEND: Strike the note and bend up 1/4 step.

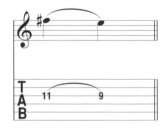

BEND AND RELEASE: Strike the note and bend up as indicated, then release back to the original note. Only the first note is struck.

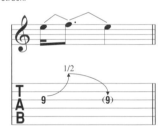

PRE-BEND: Bend the note as indicated, then strike it.

PRE-BEND AND RELEASE: Bend the note as indicated. Strike it and release the bend back to the original note.

UNISON BEND: Strike the two notes simultaneously and bend the lower note up to the pitch of the higher.

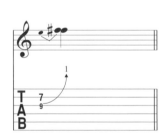

VIBRATO: The string is vibrated by rapidly bending and releasing the note with the fretting hand.

WIDE VIBRATO: The pitch is varied to a greater degree by vibrating with the fretting hand.

HAMMER-ON: Strike the first (lower) note with one finger, then sound the higher note (on the same string) with another finger by fretting it without picking.

PULL-OFF: Place both fingers on the notes to be sounded. Strike the first note and without picking, pull the finger off to sound the second (lower) note.

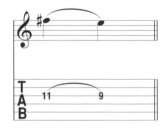

LEGATO SLIDE: Strike the first note and then slide the same fret-hand finger up or down to the second note. The second note is not struck.

SHIFT SLIDE: Same as legato slide, except the second note is struck.

TRILL: Very rapidly alternate between the notes indicated by continuously hammering on and pulling off.

TAPPING: Hammer ("tap") the fret indicated with the pick-hand index or middle finger and pull off to the note fretted by the fret hand.

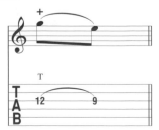

NATURAL HARMONIC: Strike the note while the fret-hand lightly touches the string directly over the fret indicated.

PINCH HARMONIC: The note is fretted normally and a harmonic is produced by adding the edge of the thumb or the tip of the index finger of the pick hand to the normal pick attack.

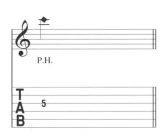

HARP HARMONIC: The note is fretted normally and a harmonic is produced by gently resting the pick hand's index finger directly above the indicated fret (in parentheses) while the pick hand's thumb or pick assists by plucking the appropriate string.

PICK SCRAPE: The edge of the pick is rubbed down (or up) the string, producing a scratchy sound.

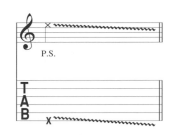

MUFFLED STRINGS: A percussive sound is produced by laying the fret hand across the string(s) without depressing, and striking them with the pick hand.

PALM MUTING: The note is partially muted by the pick hand lightly touching the string(s) just before the bridge.

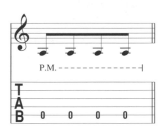

RAKE: Drag the pick across the strings indicated with a single motion.

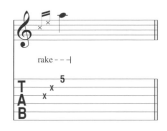

TREMOLO PICKING: The note is picked as rapidly and continuously as possible.

ARPEGGIATE: Play the notes of the chord indicated by quickly rolling them from bottom to top.

VIBRATO BAR DIVE AND RETURN: The pitch of the note or chord is dropped a specified number of steps (in rhythm), then returned to the original pitch.

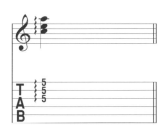

VIBRATO BAR SCOOP: Depress the bar just before striking the note, then quickly release the bar.

VIBRATO BAR DIP: Strike the note and then immediately drop a specified number of steps, then release back to the original pitch.

DEFINITIONS FOR SPECIAL GUITAR NOTATION

 *(accent)*
- Accentuate note (play it louder).

 (accent)
- Accentuate note with great intensity.

 (staccato)
- Play the note short.

- Downstroke

V
- Upstroke

D.S. al Coda
- Go back to the sign (𝄋), then play until the measure marked "*To Coda*," then skip to the section labelled "**Coda**."

D.C. al Fine
- Go back to the beginning of the song and play until the measure marked "*Fine*" (end).

Rhy. Fig.
- Label used to recall a recurring accompaniment pattern (usually chordal).

Riff
- Label used to recall composed, melodic lines (usually single notes) which recur.

Fill
- Label used to identify a brief melodic figure which is to be inserted into the arrangement.

Rhy. Fill
- A chordal version of a Fill.

tacet
- Instrument is silent (drops out).

- Repeat measures between signs.

- When a repeated section has different endings, play the first ending only the first time and the second ending only the second time.

NOTE: Tablature numbers in parentheses mean:
    1. The note is being sustained over a system (note in standard notation is tied), or
    2. The note is sustained, but a new articulation (such as a hammer-on, pull-off, slide or vibrato) begins, or
    3. The note is a barely audible "ghost" note (note in standard notation is also in parentheses).

ABOUT THE AUTHOR

FRED SOKOLOW is a versatile "musician's musician." Besides fronting his own jazz, bluegrass, and rock bands, Fred has toured with Bobbie Gentry, Jim Stafford, Tom Paxton, Ian Whitcomb, Jody Stecher, and the Limeliters, playing guitar, banjo, mandolin, and Dobro. His music has been heard on many TV shows (*Survivor*, *Dr. Quinn*), commercials, and movies (listen for his Dixieland-style banjo in *The Cat's Meow*).

Sokolow has written over a hundred fifty stringed instrument books and videos for seven major publishers. This library of instructional material, which teaches jazz, rock, bluegrass, country, and blues guitar, banjo, Dobro, ukulele, and mandolin, is sold on six continents. He also teaches musical seminars on the West Coast. Two jazz CDs, two rock guitar and two banjo recordings, which showcase Sokolow's technique, all received excellent reviews in the U.S. and Europe.

If you think Sokolow still isn't versatile enough, know that he emceed for Carol Doda at San Francisco's legendary Condor Club, accompanied a Russian balalaika virtuoso at the swank Bonaventure Hotel in L.A., won the *Gong Show*, played lap steel and banjo on the *Tonight Show*, picked Dobro with Chubby Checker, and played mandolin with Rick James.

For any questions that you may have about this book or other Fred Sokolow books, please visit www.sokolowmusic.com.

Create your own strumming and fingerpicking patterns here!

HAL LEONARD GUITAR METHOD

METHOD BOOKS, SONGBOOKS AND REFERENCE BOOKS

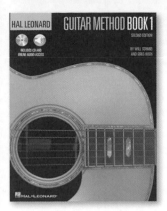

THE HAL LEONARD GUITAR METHOD is designed for anyone just learning to play acoustic or electric guitar. It is based on years of teaching guitar students of all ages, and it also reflects some of the best guitar teaching ideas from around the world. This comprehensive method includes: A learning sequence carefully paced with clear instructions; popular songs which increase the incentive to learn to play; versatility – can be used as self-instruction or with a teacher; audio accompaniments so that students have fun and sound great while practicing.

BOOK 1
00699010	Book Only	$8.99
00699027	Book/Online Audio	$12.99
00697341	Book/Online Audio + DVD	$24.99
00697318	DVD Only	$19.99
00155480	Deluxe Beginner Edition (Book, CD, DVD, Online Audio/ Video & Chord Poster)	$19.99

COMPLETE (BOOKS 1, 2 & 3)
00699040	Book Only	$16.99
00697342	Book/Online Audio	$24.99

BOOK 2
00699020	Book Only	$8.99
00697313	Book/Online Audio	$12.99

BOOK 3
00699030	Book Only	$8.99
00697316	Book/Online Audio	$12.99

Prices, contents and availability subject to change without notice.

STYLISTIC METHODS

ACOUSTIC GUITAR
00697347	Method Book/Online Audio	$17.99
00237969	Songbook/Online Audio	$16.99

BLUEGRASS GUITAR
00697405	Method Book/Online Audio	$16.99

BLUES GUITAR
00697326	Method Book/Online Audio (9" x 12")	$16.99
00697344	Method Book/Online Audio (6" x 9")	$15.99
00697385	Songbook/Online Audio (9" x 12")	$14.99
00248636	Kids Method Book/Online Audio	$12.99

BRAZILIAN GUITAR
00697415	Method Book/Online Audio	$17.99

CHRISTIAN GUITAR
00695947	Method Book/Online Audio	$16.99
00697408	Songbook/CD Pack	$14.99

CLASSICAL GUITAR
00697376	Method Book/Online Audio	$15.99

COUNTRY GUITAR
00697337	Method Book/Online Audio	$22.99
00697400	Songbook/Online Audio	$19.99

FINGERSTYLE GUITAR
00697378	Method Book/Online Audio	$21.99
00697432	Songbook/Online Audio	$16.99

FLAMENCO GUITAR
00697363	Method Book/Online Audio	$15.99

FOLK GUITAR
00697414	Method Book/Online Audio	$16.99

JAZZ GUITAR
00695359	Book/Online Audio	$22.99
00697386	Songbook/Online Audio	$15.99

JAZZ-ROCK FUSION
00697387	Book/Online Audio	$24.99

R&B GUITAR
00697356	Book/Online Audio	$19.99
00697433	Songbook/CD Pack	$14.99

ROCK GUITAR
00697319	Book/Online Audio	$16.99
00697383	Songbook/Online Audio	$16.99

ROCKABILLY GUITAR
00697407	Book/Online Audio	$16.99

OTHER METHOD BOOKS

BARITONE GUITAR METHOD
00242055	Book/Online Audio	$12.99

GUITAR FOR KIDS
00865003	Method Book 1/Online Audio	$12.99
00697402	Songbook/Online Audio	$9.99
00128437	Method Book 2/Online Audio	$12.99

MUSIC THEORY FOR GUITARISTS
00695790	Book/Online Audio	$19.99

TENOR GUITAR METHOD
00148330	Book/Online Audio	$12.99

12-STRING GUITAR METHOD
00249528	Book/Online Audio	$19.99

METHOD SUPPLEMENTS

ARPEGGIO FINDER
00697352	6" x 9" Edition	$6.99
00697351	9" x 12" Edition	$9.99

BARRE CHORDS
00697406	Book/Online Audio	$14.99

CHORD, SCALE & ARPEGGIO FINDER
00697410	Book Only	$19.99

GUITAR TECHNIQUES
00697389	Book/Online Audio	$16.99

INCREDIBLE CHORD FINDER
00697200	6" x 9" Edition	$7.99
00697208	9" x 12" Edition	$7.99

INCREDIBLE SCALE FINDER
00695568	6" x 9" Edition	$9.99
00695490	9" x 12" Edition	$9.99

LEAD LICKS
00697345	Book/Online Audio	$10.99

RHYTHM RIFFS
00697346	Book/Online Audio	$14.99

SONGBOOKS

CLASSICAL GUITAR PIECES
00697388	Book/Online Audio	$9.99

EASY POP MELODIES
00697281	Book Only	$7.99
00697440	Book/Online Audio	$14.99

(MORE) EASY POP MELODIES
00697280	Book Only	$6.99
00697269	Book/Online Audio	$14.99

(EVEN MORE) EASY POP MELODIES
00699154	Book Only	$6.99
00697439	Book/Online Audio	$14.99

EASY POP RHYTHMS
00697336	Book Only	$7.99
00697441	Book/Online Audio	$14.99

(MORE) EASY POP RHYTHMS
00697338	Book Only	$7.99
00697322	Book/Online Audio	$14.99

(EVEN MORE) EASY POP RHYTHMS
00697340	Book Only	$7.99
00697323	Book/Online Audio	$14.99

EASY POP CHRISTMAS MELODIES
00697417	Book Only	$9.99
00697416	Book/Online Audio	$14.99

EASY POP CHRISTMAS RHYTHMS
00278177	Book Only	$6.99
00278175	Book/Online Audio	$14.99

EASY SOLO GUITAR PIECES
00110407	Book Only	$9.99

REFERENCE

GUITAR PRACTICE PLANNER
00697401	Book Only	$5.99

GUITAR SETUP & MAINTENANCE
00697427	6" x 9" Edition	$14.99
00697421	9" x 12" Edition	$12.99

For more info, songlists, or to purchase these and more books from your favorite music retailer, go to

halleonard.com

HAL•LEONARD®

FINGERPICKING GUITAR BOOKS

Hone your fingerpicking skills with these great songbooks featuring solo guitar arrangements in standard notation and tablature. The arrangements in these books are carefully written for intermediate-level guitarists. Each song combines melody and harmony in one superb guitar fingerpicking arrangement. Each book also includes an introduction to basic fingerstyle guitar.

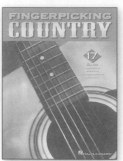

Fingerpicking Acoustic
00699614 15 songs...................... $14.99

Fingerpicking Acoustic Classics
00160211 15 songs...................... $16.99

Fingerpicking Acoustic Hits
00160202 15 songs...................... $12.99

Fingerpicking Acoustic Rock
00699764 14 songs...................... $12.99

Fingerpicking Ballads
00699717 15 songs...................... $14.99

Fingerpicking Beatles
00699049 30 songs...................... $24.99

Fingerpicking Beethoven
00702390 15 pieces..................... $9.99

Fingerpicking Blues
00701277 15 songs $10.99

Fingerpicking Broadway Favorites
00699843 15 songs...................... $9.99

Fingerpicking Broadway Hits
00699838 15 songs...................... $7.99

Fingerpicking Campfire
00275964 15 songs...................... $12.99

Fingerpicking Celtic Folk
00701148 15 songs...................... $10.99

Fingerpicking Children's Songs
00699712 15 songs...................... $9.99

Fingerpicking Christian
00701076 15 songs...................... $12.99

Fingerpicking Christmas
00699599 20 carols..................... $10.99

Fingerpicking Christmas Classics
00701695 15 songs...................... $7.99

Fingerpicking Christmas Songs
00171333 15 songs...................... $10.99

Fingerpicking Classical
00699620 15 pieces..................... $10.99

Fingerpicking Country
00699687 17 songs...................... $12.99

Fingerpicking Disney
00699711 15 songs...................... $16.99

Fingerpicking Early Jazz Standards
00276565 15 songs $12.99

Fingerpicking Duke Ellington
00699845 15 songs...................... $9.99

Fingerpicking Enya
00701161 15 songs...................... $15.99

Fingerpicking Film Score Music
00160143 15 songs...................... $12.99

Fingerpicking Gospel
00701059 15 songs...................... $9.99

Fingerpicking Hit Songs
00160195 15 songs...................... $12.99

Fingerpicking Hymns
00699688 15 hymns $12.99

Fingerpicking Irish Songs
00701965 15 songs...................... $10.99

Fingerpicking Italian Songs
00159778 15 songs...................... $12.99

Fingerpicking Jazz Favorites
00699844 15 songs...................... $12.99

Fingerpicking Jazz Standards
00699840 15 songs...................... $10.99

Fingerpicking Elton John
00237495 15 songs...................... $14.99

Fingerpicking Latin Favorites
00699842 15 songs...................... $12.99

Fingerpicking Latin Standards
00699837 15 songs...................... $15.99

Fingerpicking Andrew Lloyd Webber
00699839 14 songs...................... $16.99

Fingerpicking Love Songs
00699841 15 songs...................... $14.99

Fingerpicking Love Standards
00699836 15 songs $9.99

Fingerpicking Lullabyes
00701276 16 songs...................... $9.99

Fingerpicking Movie Music
00699919 15 songs...................... $12.99

Fingerpicking Mozart
00699794 15 pieces..................... $9.99

Fingerpicking Pop
00699615 15 songs...................... $14.99

Fingerpicking Popular Hits
00139079 14 songs...................... $12.99

Fingerpicking Praise
00699714 15 songs...................... $12.99

Fingerpicking Rock
00699716 15 songs...................... $12.99

Fingerpicking Standards
00699613 17 songs...................... $14.99

Fingerpicking Wedding
00699637 15 songs...................... $10.99

Fingerpicking Worship
00700554 15 songs...................... $14.99

Fingerpicking Neil Young – Greatest Hits
00700134 16 songs...................... $14.99

Fingerpicking Yuletide
00699654 16 songs...................... $12.99

HAL•LEONARD®
Order these and more great publications from your favorite music retailer at
halleonard.com

Prices, contents and availability subject to change without notice.

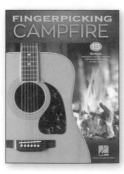